WORLD CUP 2010

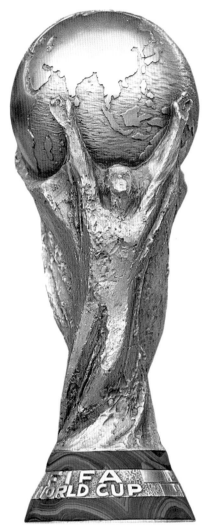

JOEL SIMONS

HERMES HOUSE

This edition is published by
Hermes House, an imprint of
Anness Publishing Ltd, Hermes House,
88–89 Blackfriars Road, London SE1 8HA
tel. 020 7401 2077; fax 020 7633 9499

www.hermeshouse.com;
www.annesspublishing.com

Anness Publishing has a new picture agency
outlet for images for publishing, promotions
or advertising. Please visit our website
www.practicalpictures.com for more information.

Publisher: Joanna Lorenz
Project Editors: Sarah Ainley and Joel Simons
Proofreading Manager: Lindsay Zamponi
Copy Editor: Jay Thundercliffe
Production Controller: Don Campaniello
Original text by Gavin Hamilton

ETHICAL TRADING POLICY

Because of our ongoing ecological investment programme, you, as our customer, can have the pleasure and reassurance of knowing that a tree is being cultivated on your behalf to naturally replace the materials used to make the book you are holding. For further information about this scheme, go to www.annesspublishing.com/trees

PUBLISHER'S NOTE

Although the advice and information in this book are believed to be accurate and true at the time of going to press, neither the authors nor the publisher can accept any legal responsibility or liability for any errors or omissions that may be made.

FIXTURES

All dates, times and locations of those World Cup fixtures listed in this volume are correct at the time of publication. However, these fixtures are subject to change. An up-to-date list will be available on the FIFA website at www.fifa.com

PICTURE CREDITS

All images supplied by Offside Sports Photography except for the following:
t = top; b = bottom; l = left; r = right; c = centre
Allsport 1c; 3bl, c; 4tr, bl, br; 5tr; 6m, tr, br; 8t, bl, br; 9t, r, bl; 10tr, bl; 11tr, bl, br; 12tr, bl; 13t, tr, bl, br; 14tl, bl, br; 15b, tr; 16tr, bl, br; 17tr, tl, b, br; 18t, tr, bl, b, br; 19t, tr, b; 29tr; 30bl; 31bl; 32tl; 33tr; 34bl; 39tr; 40tr; 44bl; 45tr, bl; 47bl; 48bl; 49t, tr; 52bl; 55bl; 58bl, tr; 64bl, t, l

Contents

Introduction	**4**
A History of the World Cup	**6**
1930s	8
1950s	10
1960s	12
1970s	14
1980s	16
1990s	18
2000s	20
2010: The Qualifiers	22
2010: Qualifying Results	24
The Teams	**26**
Group A	
South Africa	28
Mexico	29
Uruguay	30
France	31
Group B	
Argentina	32
Nigeria	33
South Korea	34
Greece	35

Group C	
England	36
USA	37
Algeria	38
Slovenia	39
Group D	
Germany	40
Australia	41
Serbia	42
Ghana	43

Group E	
Holland	44
Denmark	45
Japan	46
Cameroon	47
Group F	
Italy	48
Paraguay	49
New Zealand	50
Slovakia	51
Group G	
Brazil	52
DPR Korea	53
Ivory Coast	54
Portugal	55
Group H	
Spain	56
Switzerland	57
Chile	58
Honduras	59
World Cup 2010: Results	**60**
Index	**64**

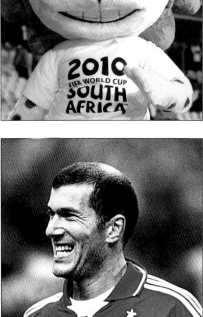

Introduction

The World Cup is, quite simply, the greatest sporting show on earth. The Olympics may be a wonderful showcase for individual talent; the Champions League may be the natural home for the aristocrats of European club football; but the World Cup beats them all. The planet's best footballers on the world's biggest stage, competing for the global game's greatest prize. Sport does not get any bigger, or any better, than that.

From humble beginnings in front of a few thousand people in Montevideo, Uruguay, in 1930, the World Cup has grown into a global television spectacle watched by billions of people around the world. A collective television audience of 715 million watched Italy's triumph in Germany four years ago. This year's finals in South Africa will be seen by an estimated 4 billion people.

South Africa 2010, the third World Cup finals of the 21st century, will be the first tournament staged in Africa following FIFA's decision to hold an all-African bidding process between Morocco, Egypt and South Africa. A total of 200 teams entered the

Below: The Brazilian team celebrate their first World Cup win in 1958.

Above: Jürgen Klinnsman, as the Germans seal their 1990 win over Italy.

Below: Diego Maradona entertained the world at the Mexico finals in 1986.

Above: Brazil win the World Cup for the fourth time in the United States in 1994.

Right: The 2006 World Champions, Italy, celebrate their win in Germany.

qualification phase in 2007 to compete for 31 places (with a place automatically taken by the host nation), with ten fantastic stadia staging the vast amount of talent. The games begin in the Soccer City Stadium in Johannesburg on 11th June 2010. A worldwide audience is then treated to games across nine host cities from Cape Town to Durban, with teams from six worldwide FIFA confederations competing to get their hands on the World Cup trophy.

In 2006, Germany hosted the tournament during a gorgeous summer heatwave. Italy, the victors in Berlin, will start as defending champions in Johannesburg and will attempt to retain the most prestigious of footballing crowns from 31 other pretenders.

A HISTORY OF THE WORLD CUP

South Africa 2010 will be the nineteenth World Cup and the first to be held on the African continent. Previous finals have been the stage for wonderful individual talent, from teenager Pelé in 1958 to Geoff Hurst's Wembley hat-trick in 1966, and the unstoppable Diego Maradona in 1986. Opinions are fierce over which tournament has been the best, which teams have shone the brightest and which giantkillers have sprung the greatest shocks. A new layer is added to the World Cup legend with each finals, and the stature of football's greatest competition grows.

1930s

The idea of a World Cup was first discussed in 1904 at the first meeting of FIFA, world football's governing body. However, the first finals were not held until 1930, in Uruguay.

1930

Thirteen teams entered the tournament in its inaugural year, and only four countries from Europe – France, Yugoslavia, Romania and Belgium – made the gruelling three-week trip by boat to South America. Italy, Holland, Spain and Sweden all stayed away, unhappy that their offers to host the finals had been rejected in favour of the Uruguayans, who offered to pay the travel and hotel costs of all the finalists. There were no British teams, the British authorities having withdrawn from FIFA in 1928 over arguments about what constituted an amateur player so far as the Olympic Games were concerned. Austria, Germany, Czechoslovakia and Switzerland also declined invitations.

Uruguay, as hosts and Olympic champions, were undoubtedly the favourites, and duly beat Peru and Romania in their pool, or group.

Below: Uruguay celebrate after beating Argentina 4–2 in the 1930 final.

France won their opening game, against Mexico, but then lost to Argentina, the eventual winners of Pool 1. Yugoslavia were the unexpected winners of Pool 2, overcoming the more talented Brazilians. In the final pool, the USA, who had a professional league staffed mainly by Englishmen and Scots, saw off Paraguay and Belgium.

However, the USA were no match for Argentina in the semi-final, and were crushed 6–1. Yugoslavia shocked Uruguay by going a goal up after four minutes of the other semi-final, but the hosts recovered to win 6–1.

For the final, Argentinian fans packed into boats and crossed the River Plate to Montevideo. Argentina were 2–1 up by half-time, but Uruguay, inspired by the inside-left Pedro Cea, recovered to win 4–2, becoming the first-ever world champions.

1934

Uruguay, still upset at the European absence in 1930, did not travel to Italy to defend their title four years later. The two South American teams that did attend, Brazil and Argentina, left after losing their first games, to Spain and Sweden respectively.

There were two clear favourites before the tournament began: Italy the hosts, managed by the charismatic

Above: Jules Rimet (left) with the first World Cup trophy, in 1930.

Vittorio Pozzo, and Austria, managed by the influential Hugo Meisl. The two teams met in the semi-finals, but the Italians were too strong and too focused for the Austrians, and they won the match 1–0. Czechoslovakia beat Germany in the other semi-final, after the Germans' game seemed to collapse in the second half, and they eventually lost the match 3–1.

Below: Vittorio Pozzo (left), manager of the Italian team in 1934.

Above: Italy's players carry manager Vittorio Pozzo aloft after victory in the 1938 World Cup final.

In the final in Rome, Italy's stamina and home support proved more of a match for the Czechs' individual skills, but the goals came late in the game. The Italians went a goal down when Puc scored, but Orsi equalized with a fabulous solo goal, and Schiavio grabbed the winner in extra time.

Below: Italy celebrate the first of their two World Cup victories in the 1930s – a win over Czechoslovakia in 1934.

1938

By the time of the 1938 finals, held in France, Italy were also the Olympic champions. However, many of the players from the victorious 1934 side had gone, although captain Giuseppe Meazza was still a key figure.

Again there were some big names missing – including Argentina and Uruguay – and there was room for the Dutch East Indies and Cuba.

Italy scored after two minutes of their opening game with Norway, but were forced into extra time when Norway

Above: Italy defender Alfredi Foni (left) in the 1938 final against Hungary.

deservedly equalized with only a few minutes remaining. Piola then scored the winner for the holders. Italy then reached the final after defeats of France (3–1) and Brazil (2–1).

In the final against Hungary, Meazza and Ferrari, Italy's two inside-forwards, controlled the game, setting up two goals apiece for Colaussi and Piola as the Italians won 4–2 and retained their World Cup title.

1950s

The first World Cup finals to be staged after the end of World War II came in 1950, ending a 12-year gap.

1950

There were only 13 finalists at the tournament in Brazil, with many key teams missing, including Argentina, Czechoslovakia, Germany (who were still banned following the war), France, Scotland, Portugal, Austria and Hungary. The Maracana stadium in Rio de Janeiro, which was built as a centrepiece for the finals and remained unfinished on the opening day, held a record 200,000 spectators.

England competed in the finals for the first time, but were subject to one of the greatest shocks in World Cup history. The team was full of talent – Stanley Matthews, Stan Mortensen, Tom Finney – but after winning their first match 2–0 against Chile, they inexplicably lost 1–0 to the United States in Belo Horizonte.

The absence of many leading teams skewed the draw in favour of Uruguay. Unlike previous finals, the 1950 tournament was settled by a pool system rather than knockout matches.

Below: The England squad arrives in Brazil ahead of the 1950 finals.

The final pool comprised the four winners of the opening pools: Brazil, Uruguay, Spain and Sweden. In fact, the pool went down to a final match, Brazil against Uruguay, so there was a kind of final after all.

Brazil expected to be crowned world champions for the first time, but Uruguay, inspired by their captain Obdulio Varela, resisted all Brazilian attacks. Friaca scored for Brazil early in the second half, but the Uruguayans equalized through Schiaffino and then grabbed a winner through Ghiggia with ten minutes remaining. Uruguay were champions for a second time.

1954

Hungary were the overwhelming favourites to win the 1954 finals, held in Switzerland. They had emerged from behind the Iron Curtain to win the 1952 Olympic title. A year later, they had stunned England at Wembley, winning 6–3 with a breathtaking display of attacking football.

There was another change in the tournament format that year, with the top two teams from each opening group going into the quarter-finals.

West Germany had not been among the pre-tournament favourites, and an 8–3 defeat by Hungary in their second

Above: West Germany's Helmut Rahn challenges Hungary's Grosics in 1954.

game did little to boost their chances. But they recovered their confidence to beat Yugoslavia in the quarter-finals and Austria in the semi-finals.

Hungary beat Brazil 4–2 in the quarter-finals, in an infamous match called the 'Battle of Berne', and then beat the holders Uruguay by the same score in a classic semi-final. Hungary welcomed back a still unfit Ferenc Puskas, badly injured against West Germany, for the final against the same opponents. Two up in eight minutes, they were pulled back to 2–2, and, although they attacked relentlessly, it was West Germany who snatched an unlikely winner through Helmut Rahn, 12 minutes from time.

The Magic Magyars
Hungary arrived for the 1954 finals in Zurich as hottest-ever tournament favourites. The trio Puskas, Hidegkuti and Kocsis brought a new dimension to the game which had already proved unbeatable at the 1952 Olympic Games in Helsinki.

1958

The 1958 finals were played in Sweden and were dominated by Brazil, who won their first World Cup. This was the year that the Brazilians, playing a new 4–2–4 system, introduced the 17-year-old Pelé to the world stage.

Pelé was, without any doubt, the star of the tournament, scoring twice as Sweden were beaten 5–2 by Brazil in the final in Stockholm. The Swedes, managed by an Englishman, George

Right: Brazil's victorious team line up with the trophy in Sweden in 1958.

Below: The teenager Pelé (right) jumps with Swedish keeper Svensson in 1958.

Raynor, had beaten holders Germany in the semi-finals, and had exceeded all expectations by reaching the final, but they were simply blown away by the brilliance of the Brazilians. Pelé, whose first goal was magical, remained the youngest World Cup player until 1982. He was in tears at the finish.

France were the other surprise team that year, finishing third thanks to the goals - 13 of them, a World Cup record that still stands - of Just Fontaine.

Below: An exuberant Brazil beat Sweden 5–2 in the final of 1958.

1960s

Brazil, with Pelé fast maturing into the greatest footballer ever seen, were a powerful force by the early 1960s.

1962

Brazil were the favourites to retain their world title at the 1962 finals in Chile, a country that had been hit by an earthquake just months before the finals. "We must have the World Cup because we have nothing", said Carlos Dittborn, president of Chilean football.

Brazil retained many of the players from their 1958 squad: Vava, Didi, Garrincha, Nilton Santos, Djalmar Santos, Gilmar and, of course, Pelé.

The Brazilians won their opening game against Mexico but were held 0–0 by the Czechs and, worst of all, lost Pelé with a torn thigh muscle. Without him, they struggled to beat Spain but reached the quarter-finals, where they faced England. Garrincha's brilliance sealed the game, as he scored twice and set up the third for Vava in a 3–1 win.

Brazil met Chile in the semi-finals, where the hosts were outplayed by the Brazilians, for whom Garrincha and Vava both scored twice.

Below: Amarildo, Brazil's opening goalscorer in the 1962 final.

In the opening round, Chile met Italy in one of the most violent World Cup matches ever, which became known as the 'Battle of Santiago'. Two Italian players were sent off as Italy lost 2–0 and crashed out.

In the quarter-final, Chile sprang a surprise by beating the USSR 2–1 after some uncharacteristic mistakes by Soviet goalkeeper Lev Yashin.

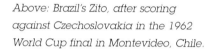

Above: Brazil's Zito, after scoring against Czechoslovakia in the 1962 World Cup final in Montevideo, Chile.

While Brazil outclassed Chile in one semi-final, the other semi was watched by just 5,000 spectators. They saw a surprise as Czechoslovakia defied the form book to beat Yugoslavia 3–1.

In the final, Czechoslovakia took a shock early lead through Josef Masopust, but Brazil quickly equalized through Amarildo, who proved an effective replacement for Pelé. Amarildo set up Brazil's second goal, a tap-in for Zito, and then a mistake by goalkeeper Schroiff gifted Vava Brazil's third.

1966

The 1966 finals in England were the first since Italy in 1934 to be won by the home nation. England's 4–2 victory over West Germany in the final at Wembley is remembered as one of the great finals, although much of the early tournament was not nearly as exciting.

Holders Brazil still had many of the players who had won them the competition in 1958 and 1962, but

they lost Pelé to injury in their opening game against Bulgaria. Without Pelé, the Brazilians were beaten by Hungary 3–1. Pelé returned against Portugal, but he was not fully fit and was injured once again as the defending champions crashed out of the tournament.

England, dubbed the Wingless Wonders, played their group games at Wembley. They stayed in London for their quarter-final against Argentina – a bitter match in which Argentina's captain was sent off. England won 1–0. Without Brazil, Portugal, with Eusebio and other stars from Benfica's 1962 European Cup-winning side, looked likely contenders. They beat North Korea 5–3 in the quarter-finals to book a semi-final place against England.

The North Koreans had earlier provided the shock of the tournament when they beat Italy 1–0.

The two semi-final matches were very different. In one, West Germany, featuring a young Franz Beckenbauer, beat the Soviet Union 2–1 in a poor, ill-disciplined game. In the other, England's contest came alive with a

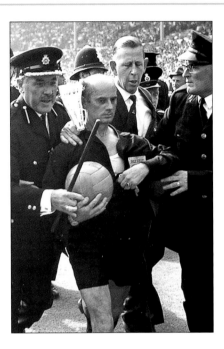

Above: Referee Ken Aston with police protection after the 'Battle of Santiago'.

2–1 win over Portugal. Bobby Charlton was outstanding for England, scoring a spectacular long-range shot; Nobby Stiles cancelled out Portugal's Eusebio.

Geoff Hurst, preferred to Jimmy Greaves, was England's hero in the final against West Germany, scoring a hat-trick, including two goals in extra time. Hurst's second goal, and

Above: Eusebio, an inspiration for the Portuguese side at the 1966 finals.

England's third, was widely disputed by the Germans, who were unhappy at the Russian linesman's insistence that the ball had crossed the line. But there was no disputing a thumping fourth goal in England's 4–2 victory.

Below: England's disputed third goal in the 1966 final against West Germany.

Below: England celebrate victory over the Germans at Wembley in 1966.

1970s

The England side remained a force to be reckoned with after their 1966 victory, but had peaked by the time the finals came round four years later.

1970

The 1970 finals, played in Mexico, are famous for the magical Brazilian side that beat Italy 4–1 in the final.

That year, Brazil became the first team ever to win the World Cup final three times and keep the Jules Rimet trophy on a permanent basis. With a forward line of Pelé, Tostão, Jairzinho and Rivelino, and midfielders Gerson and Clodoaldo, it mattered little that their defence was poor or that their goalkeeper Felix was especially weak.

Brazil played England in the opening group, a match seen by many as the real final: the holders v the favourites. Early in the game, England keeper Gordon Banks pulled off one of the greatest saves ever from Pelé, but England missed chances and eventually Jairzinho scored the game's only goal.

Below: The Azteca stadium, Mexico City, venue for the final of 1970.

England went on to meet West Germany in the quarter-finals, this time without Banks, who had been taken ill. England controlled the game for an hour, going 2–0 up before wilting in the heat and allowing Germany to pull level. In extra time, Gerd Müller, known as 'Der Bomber', volleyed in Germany's winner.

In the semi-finals, the Germans fell to Italy in a dramatic match, which ended 4–3 after extra time, while Brazil defeated Uruguay 3–1.

In the final, the Brazilians produced a wonderful display of attacking football against a sterile, defensive Italy. A 4–1 victory was sealed three minutes from time with a marvellous goal from their captain, Carlos Alberto.

1974

The 1974 finals, held in West Germany, will be remembered as the World Cup of 'Total Football'. The German hosts beat Holland 2–1 in the final, but many felt that the best team had not won.

The Dutch team, inspired by Johan Cruyff, Johan Neeskens and other members of the Ajax side that had won the European Cup for three successive seasons, played some enchanting football on their way to the final. The essence of Holland's game was that

Above: Germany's Franz Beckenbauer lifts the World Cup trophy in 1974.

Below: Johan Cruyff (left) and Johan Neeskens of the 1974 Holland side.

Total Football

The concept of rotation play, known as Total Football, was designed to replace the more rigid play of 4-2-4 and 4-3-3. Dutch coach, Rinus Michels, was responsible for the idea, and he showed it to the world with the Holland side of 1974.

all their players were interchangeable. It was not a new philosophy, but it was wonderfully executed by the Dutch.

Brazil, without Pelé (now retired) and the injured Tostão, adopted a negative approach to their meeting with Holland in their final round group and lost to superb goals from Cruyff and Neeskens.

In the other group, West Germany beat Poland 1–0, but only after crucial saves from the German keeper Sepp Maier. The Poles, the reigning Olympic champions, beat Brazil for third place.

The final took an extraordinary turn in the opening minute, when Cruyff won a penalty, converted by Neeskens. Such an early goal demanded a response from the Germans, who scored through Breitner (another penalty) and, inevitably, Müller. Their captain Franz Beckenbauer, outstanding throughout as an attacking sweeper, lifted the trophy for the hosts.

1978

The 1978 finals were held in Argentina, despite concerns about the country's military junta. In a re-run of the previous tournament four years earlier, the hosts triumphed over Holland in the final. Unlucky Holland have still to win the World Cup.

There were some notable absentees: Johan Cruyff refused to travel with Holland, while West Germany were without Franz Beckenbauer, Gerd Müller and Wolfgang Overath.

Argentina did not recall many of their European-based players; one exception was Mario Kempes, who was to be Argentina's hero in the final in Buenos Aires, scoring twice, including the crucial second goal in extra time as the hosts beat Holland 3–1.

The Dutch had again come very close to winning the World Cup. After Kempes had given Argentina the lead in the first half, Holland dominated the second half and equalized through Dirk Nanninga. In the very last minute, Rob Rensenbrink was played through on goal but hit a post. Thus, Holland, the best team in the world, narrowly missed out again.

Italy and Brazil, teams in transition at that time, met in the third-place play-off, won 2–1 by the Brazilians.

Above: A ticker-tape reception for Argentina in Buenos Aires in 1978.

Below: Argentina celebrate victory over Holland in the 1978 final.

1980s

With a greater number of teams than ever, FIFA had once again to make adjustments to the competition format.

1982

The 1982 finals were held in Spain and the number of finalists was increased from 16 to 24, which meant that many new sides from outside Europe and South America competed in the finals for the first time. They included New Zealand, Kuwait, Honduras, El Salvador, Algeria and Cameroon.

But in the end it was one of the traditional powers of world football that triumphed in the final in Madrid's Bernabeu stadium. Italy had been unimpressive in their early matches, failing to win any of their opening group games. But their canny coach, Enzo Bearzot, was able to call upon the opportunistic striking talent of Paolo Rossi, who had recently returned from a two-year ban following his involvement in an Italian match-fixing scandal.

Rossi emerged as the star of the finals, scoring a hat-trick in the match of the tournament, Italy's 3–2 defeat of Brazil

Below: Paolo Rossi, Italy's goalscoring hero, in the 1982 finals in Spain.

in the second round, as well as two goals in Italy's semi-final win over Poland and the opening goal in their final against West Germany.

Before their defeat by Italy, Brazil had been playing some delightful football and were rightly the favourites to reach the final. But as attractive as the football played by Zico, Falcão and Socrates was, they were no match for Rossi the goal-poacher.

Hosts Spain struggled to live up to their billing as the pre-tournament favourites. They lost to Northern Ireland in the last match of their first-round group and were overwhelmed by West Germany in the second round to finish bottom of their group.

West Germany had several talented players in Karl-Heinz Rummenigge, Hansi Müller and Jorst Hrubesch. But they won few friends in their semi-final victory over France, on penalties in extra time, when a disabling tackle by

Above: Italy celebrate victory over West Germany in the 1982 World Cup.

Below: Diego Maradona takes on Belgium single-handed in 1982.

Above: England's Gary Lineker hits a hat-trick against Poland in 1986.

Harald 'Toni' Schumacher on Patrick Battiston went unpunished. Neutrals were delighted when Italy beat West Germany 3–1 in the final, Italy's third World Cup triumph.

1986

Doubts about Colombia's ability to host a World Cup tournament forced FIFA to switch the 1986 finals to Mexico, a country still recovering from a tragic earthquake.

One man dominated the tournament that year: Diego Armando Maradona. The diminutive Argentinian was the outstanding player of the tournament. He inspired Argentina to victory over West Germany in the final, after scoring two brilliant solo goals against England and Belgium, and causing a storm of controversy with his 'Hand of God'.

In Argentina's quarter-final match against England, Maradona used his hand to punch the ball past goalkeeper Peter Shilton and into the net. He later denied cheating, saying the goal was legitimate because he had been assisted by the 'Hand of God'. But there could be no doubt about the brilliance of his second goal; Maradona collected the ball in his own half, beat five English defenders and slid the ball past Shilton. He repeated the feat with a similar goal in the semi-final against Belgium.

In the final in Mexico City against West Germany, Maradona was more subdued but he still laid on the pass for Jorge Burruchaga to score the winning goal. Argentina had gone 2–0 up through Jose-Luis Brown and Jorge Valdano, only for the Germans to draw level, with Karl-Heinz Rummenigge and Rudi Völler scoring from corners.

Argentina had won their second World Cup playing an innovative 3–5–2 formation with wing-backs, a tactic that would be widely copied.

The match of the tournament was France's quarter-final defeat of Brazil on penalties, after a 1–1 draw.

Below: French midfield star, Michel Platini, scores against Brazil in 1986.

Above: Mexico's Hugo Sanchez gets booked in front of a home crowd, 1986.

Below: Diego Maradona collects the 1986 World Cup trophy for Argentina.

1990s

The World Cup continued to grow in the last decade of the century. By the 1998 finals, in France, the event had expanded to accommodate 32 finalists.

1990

Germany were victorious at Italia 1990, winning their third World Cup after beating Argentina 1–0 in the final in Rome's Stadio Olimpico. The match was a personal triumph for manager Franz Beckenbauer, who became the first person to captain and coach World Cup-winning sides.

The final itself was an anti-climax, however. Argentina had two men sent off and were beaten by a late penalty from Andreas Brehme.

The tournament as a whole was criticized for being too defensive, with both semi-finals going to penalties, but there were some notable highlights. Costa Rica stunned Scotland and Sweden to reach the second round. Cameroon, inspired by 42-year-old Roger Milla, beat the holders Argentina in the opening match and then ran England close in a pulsating quarter-final. England played out another epic in their semi-final against Germany, agonizingly losing on penalties in a

Above: Jung Won Seo, of South Korea, gets an equalizer against Spain, 1994.

Left: Cameroon, one of the big surprises of the tournament in Italy in 1990.

game now infamous for the tears of a young Paul Gascoigne. Hosts Italy unearthed a hero in striker Salvatore 'Toto' Schillaci, the tournament's top scorer, but could not find a way past Argentina in their semi-final in Naples.

It was to be Germany's tournament, especially after they had seen off the challenge of European champions Holland in the second round.

1994

The first finals to be staged in North America were a huge success, with plenty of attacking football and huge crowds packing out the stadiums.

Brazil may have lacked some of the qualities of previous Brazilian sides, but they were inspired by striker Romario, the player of the tournament. They claimed a record fourth World Cup

Below: Paul Gascoigne, a sentimental star for England at Italia 1990.

Below: Toto Schillaci, tournament top scorer and unlikely Italian hero in 1990.

Below: Romania's Gheorghe Hagi, an inspiration for his country at USA 1994.

Above: Baby celebration to honour the goal of Brazil's Bebeto (centre) in 1994.

after winning the first final settled on penalties. They drew 0–0 with Italy in the blazing heat of the Pasadena Rose Bowl, in California, and they held their nerve in the shoot-out.

USA 1994 produced some unlikely heroes – notably Gheorghe Hagi of Romania, Oleg Salenko, a five-goal hero in Russia's 6–1 mauling of Cameroon, and Saudi Arabia's Saeed Al-Owairan, scorer of an amazing solo goal against Belgium. Bulgaria, inspired by Hristo Stoichkov, pulled off the shock of the tournament when they beat holders Germany 2–1, but in the semi-finals they lost 2–0 to a Roberto Baggio-inspired Italy.

And of course there were villains, not least the Argentine hero of 1986, Diego Maradona, who failed a drugs test and left the tournament in disgrace.

The biggest tragedy was suffered by Colombia, whose defender Andes Escobar, scorer of an own goal against the USA, was shot dead by one of his countrymen on his return home.

Right: French midfielder Zinedine Zidane scores against an unfocused Brazil in the World Cup final of 1998.

1998

France became the first hosts to win the World Cup since Argentina in 1978, when they beat Brazil 3–0 at Stade de France in Paris. But the final was overshadowed by the mystery surrounding the appearance of Brazilian striker Ronaldo. The world's most famous player had reportedly suffered a convulsive fit hours before the final, but he was cleared to play. His lack of fitness clearly affected his team-mates, who capitulated in the most one-sided final of recent years.

France were worthy world champions, however. In Zinedine Zidane, scorer of two headed goals in the final, they had

Above: Croatia's Davor Suker was top scorer at the finals in France in 1998.

one of the world's greatest midfield playmakers, although they lacked punch in attack.

Croatia, making their first World Cup appearance, were the surprise team that year, beating Holland for third place, with striker Davor Suker finishing as top scorer. Holland, once again, played some of the best football, including the goal of the tournament by Dennis Bergkamp in the quarter-final against Argentina, who earlier had conceded another great goal, by Michael Owen, in beating England 2–1.

2000s

With the ever-increasing interest in club football throughout the world, FIFA chose to hold the opening World Cup of the new millennium in Asia for the first time in the tournament's history.

2002

The first World Cup of the new century was significant for two reasons: it was the first FIFA tournament to be co-hosted between two countries and it was the first World Cup to be held in Asia. The eventual co-hosts were Japan and South Korea, who had originally applied separately to host the tournament but decided in the last minute to join forces to increase their chances of selection.

Below: Co-hosts South Korea reach the 2002 World Cup semi-final.

The opening game set a precedent for the remainder of the tournament, namely one of shocking results. The 1998 champions France were taken apart by debutants Senegal, losing 1–0 to the West Africans before eventually exiting the tournament without scoring a single goal. Portugal were also early group victims, stunned by the USA who beat them 3–2 in their opening fixture in Suwon, South Korea.

Brazil and Spain, meanwhile, cruised out of their groups with maximum points and looked on course to meet in an entertaining final. That wasn't to be, however, as South Korea bettered Korea DPR's feat set 40 years earlier by becoming the only Asian team to reach a World Cup semi-final, beating Spain on penalties in a nail-biting quarter-final in Grangju, South Korea. Brazil

Above: The top World Cup goalscorer of all time, Ronaldo, admires the view.

beat a disappointing England 2–0 in the quarter-final, with Ronaldinho lobbing England goalkeeper David Seaman from 42 yards in one of the best goals of the tournament.

The final was a return of sorts for Brazilian legend Ronaldo, who scored 2 of his record-breaking 15 World Cup goals in the final against Germany at the International Stadium in Yokohama, Japan. The Brazilian was awarded the coveted Golden Boot after the game – which Brazil won 2–0 – and consigned bitter memories of France 1998 to dust.

The tournament was also notable for its extraordinary third-place play-off game between South Korea and Turkey in which Hakan Sukur scored the fastest World Cup goal of all time, netting 11 seconds after kick-off.

2006

The eighteenth FIFA World Cup was held during a glorious heatwave in Germany in the summer of 2006. The tournament was hailed by many as one

of the best yet and was certainly one of the most successful in terms of worldwide television ratings.

The tournament began fantastically, as the hosts Germany took on Costa Rica, beating 'Los Ticas' 4–2 in the highest-scoring opening match in World Cup history. Group C, nicknamed the 'group of death', was perhaps the most entertaining, with both Holland and the impressive Argentina escaping their group with ease. Perhaps the most significant result, however, was Ghana's 2–1 win against the USA, which guaranteed Africa only its third-ever representative in the World Cup knockout stages, following the swashbuckling Cameroon in 1990 and Senegal in 2002.

The freewheeling nature of the opening games didn't continue, however, as many teams cancelled each other out: Portugal and England both edged through to meet in the quarter-finals, beating Holland and Ecuador respectively. The game followed a familiar pattern for England, with a nail-biting finish

Below: French playmaker Zinedine Zidane during the infamous 2006 final.

followed by defeat in a penalty shoot-out. Switzerland, meanwhile, became the only team not to concede a goal in the competition, though their loss to Ukraine on penalties in the second round hardly represented a great achievement.

Having cruised through the second round, France met Brazil in the quarter-final in a replay of the 1998 final; it was a tight game, with Thierry Henry grabbing the only goal to send the South Americans out of the tournament and, with Argentina losing to Germany on penalties, the win guaranteed an all-European final.

Indeed, the final was played between two European giants of world football, France and Italy. Having knocked the favourites and host nation Germany out in the semi-final, Italy looked to become the most successful international team in Europe by winning their fourth World Cup title.

Above: Italy's goalkeeper Gianluigi Buffon celebrates World Cup victory.

France, meanwhile, were full of self-belief following tough assignments against both Brazil and Portugal, and looked to repeat the success of Paris 1998 eight years later in Berlin.

The game itself was full of incident: French playmaker (and eventual Golden Ball winner) Zinedine Zidane scored a splendid penalty that cannoned off the bar, before Italy equalized with a stunning header from Marco Materazzi. As the game entered extra time, however, the two goalscorers were involved in an off-ball incident which saw Zidane sent off. Italy eventually won the final on penalties after David Trezeguet missed the target, in what was perhaps one of the most enthralling finals in recent World Cup memory.

2010: The Qualifiers

The qualifiers for South Africa 2010 produced some shocks for established footballing teams, as well as surprises from previously unheralded nations.

Asia (AFC)

The Asian qualifying section provided the first qualifiers for the 2010 finals. Australia and Japan both cruised through to the finals in the summer of 2009, finishing as winner and runner-up respectively in Group A in the final round. Group B, however, provided a few more surprises: both South Korea and Korea DPR qualified for the World Cup finals for the first time in the tournament's history. Korea DPR last qualified in 1966 when they managed to progress to the quarter-finals; South Korea, meanwhile, bettered their neighbours in 2002 by finishing fourth. Both teams booked their places in the finals by taking the top two spots in Group B of the final round of AFC qualification, while Bahrain beat Saudi Arabia (in a third-place play-off) to set up a final play-off against New Zealand, winner of the OFC zone.

Below: New Zealand's Rory Fallon netted the winner against Bahrain.

Africa (CAF)

With South Africa qualifying as host, the rest of Africa had to compete for five remaining automatic finals places.

Ghana were the first to qualify as winners of CAF Group D. Ivory Coast joined their neighbours soon after, qualifying as Group E winners in October 2009. Cameroon and Nigeria both booked their places at the tournament following victories in their final group games in November 2009. Meanwhile, Algeria were forced to play a tie-break play-off against rivals Egypt after both teams finished top of Group C.

North, Central American, and Caribbean (CONCACAF)

In Central and North America, the United States and Mexico dominated the qualifying group, taking two of the three World Cup berths. The third guaranteed finals place was claimed by Honduras, who qualified for their first tournament since 1982.

Costa Rica, meanwhile, progressed to face Uruguay in the intercontinental play-off for the final World Cup spot.

Europe (UEFA)

In the European section, nine groups produced nine automatic qualifiers and eight runners-up for the play-offs. Holland had perhaps the easiest passage, booking their place over a year before the finals began. Euro 2008 winners Spain were the strongest qualifiers, winning every game and not dropping a point in the process. England also had a surprisingly comfortable qualifying campaign, winning all but one of their games and guaranteeing their place with two games to spare under new manager Fabio Capello.

Portugal and France both struggled in their qualifying groups: they finished second to Switzerland and Serbia respectively, and entered the dreaded European play-off draw for the final few places at the finals.

Above: John Terry, key defensive player of the group-winning England side.

Oceania (OFC)

The OFC qualification group is the only confederation not to have an automatic qualifying berth for the finals. Australia's move to the AFC qualification group, however, allowed smaller teams from the region to compete for the single play-off spot.

New Zealand were the overall winners, dominating a group that contained New Caledonia, Fiji, and Vanuatu; the 'All Whites' progressed to the play-off, where they met Bahrain, the fifth-placed team in the AFC group.

South America (CONMEBOL)

For the second time in World Cup qualifying, South America's ten countries played in a single group, each playing 18 matches. Unsurprisingly, Brazil were the first to qualify from the group, losing only twice under former World Cup winner Dunga. They were duly followed by Chile and Paraguay, each of whom had respectable qualifying campaigns.

Above: Felipe Melo was an integral part of Brazil's qualification matches.

South Africa at France's expense. It was not to be, however, as French striker Thierry Henry, in the dying minutes of extra time, leapt into the six-yard box following a French free kick and handled the ball before passing it to William Gallas, who tapped the ball home. Despite the Irish protestations, his goal ensured French participation in South Africa in 2010.

Controversy also prevailed in the play-off game between Costa Rica and Uruguay when a legitimate Costa Rica goal was denied following a questionable offside decision. Despite calls for replays for both the Ireland and Costa Rica games, Uruguay joined France, Portugal and Greece in heading to South Africa for the World Cup finals in 2010. Slovenia also booked their places in the competition,

surprisingly knocking out Euro 2008 semi-finalists Russia on the away goals rule and progressing to only their second-ever appearance in a World Cup finals. New Zealand, meanwhile, also booked their second appearance at the tournament, beating Bahrain 1–0 following Rory Fallon's goal on home turf in Wellington.

Finally, Algeria and Egypt met at a neutral venue in Sudan in November 2009 to decide the winner of their CAF qualification group. Algeria won the tie 1–0, following Antar Yahia's first-half strike, as crowd trouble marred a tight contest between two very bitter rivals.

Below: Xavi Hernandez was a constant presence in midfield during Spain's perfect qualifying campaign.

Argentina's struggle to qualify was the story on everybody's lips. Having failed to qualify only once in their glorious history, Diego Maradona's team lost six matches in this campaign, including defeats against Colombia, Bolivia, Ecuador and Chile and frustrating draws against Brazil, Paraguay and Peru. Argentina qualified in fourth place, just edging out Uruguay, who entered the play-offs.

Play-offs

The play-offs for the final places in the World Cup in South Africa contained the usual controversies always apparent at the end of a long, hard World Cup qualification campaign. There were four UEFA play-off games, the most notable of which was the Republic of Ireland's two-legged contest against former world champions France. Trailing 1–0 from the first leg, Ireland travelled to Paris hoping to score an all-important away goal and perhaps book their place at the finals in

2010: Qualifying Results

AFRICA (★ denotes qualification)

Group A

	P	W	D	L	F	A	Pts
Cameroon★	6	4	1	1	9	2	13
Gabon	6	3	0	3	9	7	9
Togo	6	2	2	2	3	7	8
Morocco	6	0	3	3	3	8	3

Group B

	P	W	D	L	F	A	Pts
Nigeria★	6	3	3	0	9	4	12
Tunisia	6	3	2	1	7	4	11
Mozambique	6	2	1	3	3	5	7
Kenya	6	1	0	5	5	11	3

Group C

	P	W	D	L	F	A	Pts
Algeria★	6	4	1	1	9	4	13
Egypt	6	4	1	1	9	4	13
Zambia	6	1	2	3	2	5	5
Rwanda	6	0	2	4	1	8	2

Group D

	P	W	D	L	F	A	Pts
Ghana★	6	4	1	1	9	3	13
Benin	6	3	1	2	6	6	10
Mali	6	2	3	1	8	7	9
Sudan	6	0	1	5	2	9	1

Group E

	P	W	D	L	F	A	Pts
Ivory Coast★	6	5	1	0	19	4	16
Burkina Faso	6	4	0	2	10	11	12
Malawi	6	1	1	4	4	11	4
Guinea	6	1	0	5	7	14	3

ASIA

Group A

	P	W	D	L	F	A	Pts
Australia★	8	6	2	0	12	1	20
Japan★	8	4	3	1	11	6	15
Bahrain	8	3	1	4	6	8	10
Qatar	8	1	3	4	5	14	6
Uzbekistan	8	1	1	6	5	10	4

Group B

	P	W	D	L	F	A	Pts
South Korea★	8	4	4	0	12	4	16
Korea DPR★	8	3	3	2	7	5	12
Saudi Arabia	8	3	3	2	8	8	12
Iran	8	2	5	1	8	7	11
UAE	8	0	1	7	6	17	1

CONCACAF

	P	W	D	L	F	A	Pts
USA★	10	6	2	2	19	13	20
Mexico★	10	6	1	3	18	12	19
Honduras★	10	5	1	4	17	11	16
Costa Rica	10	5	1	4	15	15	16
El Salvador	10	2	2	6	9	15	8
Trin. & Tob.	10	1	3	6	10	22	6

OCEANIA

	P	W	D	L	F	A	Pts
N. Zealand★	6	5	0	1	14	5	15
N. Caledonia	6	2	2	2	12	10	8
Fiji	6	2	1	3	8	11	7
Vanuatu	6	1	1	4	5	13	4

(winner played AFC fifth-placed team)

SOUTH AMERICA

	P	W	D	L	F	A	Pts
Brazil★	18	9	7	2	33	11	34
Chile★	18	10	3	5	32	22	33
Paraguay★	18	10	3	5	24	16	33
Argentina★	18	8	4	6	23	20	28
Uruguay★	18	6	6	6	28	20	24
Ecuador	18	6	5	7	22	26	23
Colombia	18	6	5	7	14	18	23
Venezuela	18	6	4	8	23	29	22
Bolivia	18	4	3	11	22	36	15
Peru	18	3	4	11	11	34	13

EUROPE

Group 1

	P	W	D	L	F	A	Pts
Denmark★	10	6	3	1	16	5	21
Portugal★	10	5	4	1	17	5	19
Sweden	10	5	3	2	13	5	18
Hungary	10	5	1	4	10	8	16
Albania	10	1	4	5	6	13	7
Malta	10	0	1	9	0	26	1

Group 2

	P	W	D	L	F	A	Pts
Switzerland★	10	6	3	1	18	8	21
Greece★	10	6	2	2	20	10	20
Latvia	10	5	2	3	18	15	17
Israel	10	4	4	2	20	10	16
Luxembourg	10	1	2	7	4	25	5
Moldova	10	0	3	7	6	18	3

Below: Official posters from previous World Cup finals, including England 1966.

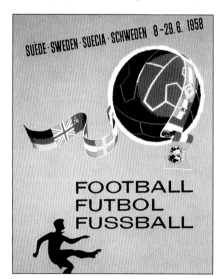

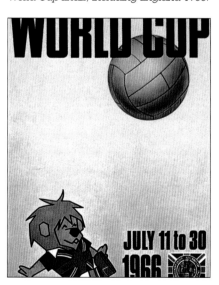

Group 3

	P	W	D	L	F	A	Pts
Slovakia★	10	7	1	2	22	10	22
Slovenia★	10	6	2	2	18	4	20
Czech Rep.	10	4	4	2	17	6	16
N. Ireland	10	4	3	3	13	9	15
Poland	10	3	2	5	19	14	11
San Marino	10	0	0	10	1	47	0

Group 4

	P	W	D	L	F	A	Pts
Germany★	10	8	2	0	26	5	26
Russia	10	7	1	2	19	6	22
Finland	10	5	3	2	14	14	18
Wales	10	4	0	6	9	12	12
Azerbaijan	10	1	2	7	4	14	5
Liechtenstein	10	0	2	8	2	23	2

Above and below: Posters from iconic World Cup finals such as Spain 1982.

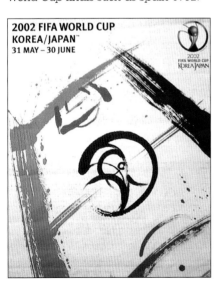

Group 5

	P	W	D	L	F	A	Pts
Spain★	10	10	0	0	28	5	30
Bosnia-Herz.	10	6	1	3	25	13	19
Turkey	10	4	3	3	13	10	15
Belgium	10	3	1	6	13	20	10
Estonia	10	2	2	6	9	24	8
Armenia	10	1	1	8	6	22	4

Group 6

	P	W	D	L	F	A	Pts
England★	10	9	0	1	34	6	27
Ukraine	10	6	3	1	21	6	21
Croatia	10	6	2	2	19	13	20
Belarus	10	4	1	5	19	14	13
Kazahkstan	10	2	0	8	11	29	6
Andorra	10	0	0	10	3	39	0

Below: 200 teams competed to qualify for the World Cup finals in South Africa

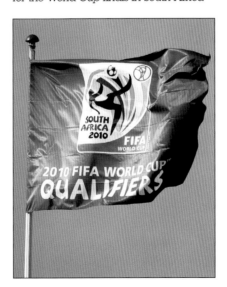

Group 7

	P	W	D	L	F	A	Pts
Serbia★	10	7	1	2	22	8	22
France★	10	6	3	1	18	9	21
Austria	10	4	2	4	14	15	14
Lithuania	10	4	0	6	10	11	12
Romania	10	3	3	4	12	18	12
Faroe Islands	10	1	1	8	5	20	4

Group 8

	P	W	D	L	F	A	Pts
Italy★	10	7	3	0	18	7	24
Rep. Ireland	10	4	6	0	12	8	18
Bulgaria	10	3	5	2	17	13	14
Cyprus	10	2	3	5	14	16	9
Montenegro	10	1	6	3	9	14	9
Gerogia	10	0	3	7	7	19	3

Group 9

	P	W	D	L	F	A	Pts
Holland★	8	8	0	0	17	2	24
Norway	8	2	4	2	9	7	10
Scotland	8	3	1	4	6	11	10
Macedonia	8	2	1	5	5	11	7
Iceland	8	1	2	5	7	13	5

PLAY-OFFS (aggregate scores)

France 2 Republic of Ireland 1
Portugal 2 Bosnia and Herzegovina 0
Greece 1 Ukraine 0
Slovenia 2 Russia 2
(Slovenia progress on away goals rule)
New Zealand 1 Bahrain 0
Uruguay 2 Costa Rica 1

THE TEAMS

Thirty-two teams will contest the 2010 World Cup finals: 13 from Europe, 5 from South America, 6 from Africa, 4 from Asia, 3 from North/Central America and 1 from Oceania. Spain, the European Champions, and Brazil, runaway winners of the South American qualifiers, start as clear favourites. Italy, England and Germany will all be confident of building on successful qualifying campaigns. Yet World Cups always produce the unexpected, and talented underdogs from across the world, such as Ghana, Chile, the USA, Slovakia and Australia, will aim to supply the surprise element. Meanwhile, many will hope to see the first African team emerge victorious at the inaugural World Cup tournament held on the African continent.

South Africa

World Cup Appearances: *2 (1998, 2002)*

World Cup Record: *First round 2 (1998, 2002)*

How They Qualified:
Automatically as hosts

Shirt: *Yellow with green trim*

It was a glorious moment in football history when, on 15th May 2004, FIFA president Sepp Blatter announced South Africa as the winner of FIFA's selection process for the host of the 2010 World Cup. Domestic and international football has a troubled history in South Africa but, despite its problems, it remains the country's most popular sport. For much of the 20th century the game was, like everything else in South Africa, blighted by apartheid, and for 28 years the South African FA was excluded from FIFA. A multiracial national team, known as Bafana Bafana ('the boys'), finally emerged from the post-apartheid South Africa in 1992 and quickly made an impact. The decision to award the World Cup rights for 2010 to South Africa was thus met with great acclaim worldwide and duly celebrated as the first World Cup to take place on African shores.

The FA of South Africa was founded in 1893, but it was only during the 1940s that the country fell in love with the game. The South African FA was represented at the 1957 meeting that led to the first African Nations Cup, but the South Africans did not participate in that year's tournament after the Confederation of African Football (CAF) made it clear that it would accept only multiracial teams. Seven years later, the SAFA was suspended by FIFA.

South Africa's return to international football in the early 1990s began inauspiciously, with the fledgling Bafana Bafana failing to qualify for either the 1994 World Cup finals or African Nations Cup finals. Two years later came better fortune when, following Kenya's decision to withdraw as hosts from the Nations Cup, South Africa filled the breach and put on a memorable show. A 3–0 victory over Ghana booked the debutants a place in the final, which was played in front of Nelson Mandela in Johannesburg, and the trophy was clinched with two goals from Mark Williams in a win against Tunisia.

In 1998, South Africa, coached by Frenchman Philippe Troussier, progressed to a second Nations Cup final, but this time they lost to Egypt in Burkina Faso. Four months later, Troussier's team, which included European-based players Mark Fish, Lucas Radebe and Benni McCarthy, competed in their first World Cup finals at France 1998. Confidence was high, but expectations were unrealistic and South Africa fell at the first hurdle. After reaching the Nations Cup semi-finals in 2000, they qualified for the World Cup finals of 2002, under Carlos Queiroz.

They beat Slovenia, but Paraguay prevented them reaching the second round by scoring one goal more.

South Africa failed to qualify for the World Cup finals in Germany 2006. Following their successful bid to host the next World Cup, South Africa also hosted the 'dress rehearsal' for the tournament, namely FIFA's Confederations Cup, which is contested by the winners of FIFA's six world confederations championships – CAF, CONMEBOL, UEFA, AFC, OFC, CONCACAF – and also includes the World Cup holders and World Cup hosts to be. South Africa faired well, finishing fourth after losing to eventual winners Brazil in the semi-final.

Below: Siphiwe Tshabalala takes on Brazil at the Confederations Cup 2009.

Mexico

World Cup Appearances: *13 (1930, 50, 54, 58, 62, 66, 70, 78, 86, 94, 98, 2002, 06)*

World Cup Record*: Quarter-finals 2 (1970, 86)*

How They Qualified: *Second place CONCACAF*

Shirt: *Green*

Mexico are one of the strongest teams of CONCACAF (North and Central America and the Caribbean), where their regional strength is so great that the nation's qualification for the World Cup finals has become almost a formality.

The Mexicans qualified for two of the three finals held during the 1990s, a decade during which they also won three out of four CONCACAF Gold Cups. In 1993 Mexico were invited to compete in the Copa America. It was a challenge that they rose to in fine style, reaching the final against Argentina, who scored a late goal to win 2–1. Mexico have continued to participate in the Copa America, achieving second place in 2001.

Mexico have enjoyed their greatest World Cup successes, unsurprisingly, on the two occasions that they hosted the competition. In 1970 they escaped their group but floundered against eventual runners-up Italy in the quarter-finals.

Sixteen years later, the Mexicans, who conceded just one goal in their five matches at the World Cup finals of 1986, were one of the tournament's more entertaining sides, and in Hugo Sanchez they possessed its most flamboyant talent. Sanchez is still regarded as Mexico's finest-ever player, and on home soil he inspired his team to a quarter-final showdown with West Germany. The match proved tense and, in the overwhelming heat of Monterrey, the Germans triumphed in a penalty shoot-out.

In 1990, Mexico's World Cup campaign ended before it had started, with the team barred from competing at the finals in Italy owing to a breach of rules at a previous youth competition. There have been other problems too, most notably at

the 1999 Copa America in Paraguay, where the achievements of the team were undermined by allegations of drug taking. Under coach Javier Aguirre, they also performed well in the 2002 World Cup finals in Japan and South Korea, winning their group before losing to the USA in the second round knockout game. They again reached the knockout stages in 2006, but a stunning extra-time volley from Argentina's Maxi Rodriguez eliminated them from the tournament.

Above: The extraordinarily gifted Hugo Sanchez went on to coach Mexico between 2006 and 2008.

Hugo Sanchez led Mexico to third place in the 2007 Copa America before the former international was sacked by the Mexican FA following a poor run of results. Javier Aguirre was re-hired in 2008 and Mexico went on to book a place at the 2010 World Cup finals by finishing second in the qualification rounds.

Uruguay

World Cup Appearances: *10 (1930, 50, 54, 62, 66, 70, 74, 86, 90, 2002)*
World Cup Record: *Winners 2 (1930, 50); fourth place 2 (1954, 70)*
How They Qualified: *Winners CONMEBOL play-off*
Shirt: *Light blue*

Uruguay are too often the forgotten World Cup winners, frequently overlooked and underestimated when the great teams of the past are reviewed and recalled. For the record, Uruguay were among the world's finest teams prior to World War II, first winning the Jules Rimet trophy in 1930. They lifted the World Cup again in 1950 and, while they have ceased to be serious contenders for the game's top prize since the 1970s, their past achievements are worthy of greater recognition. Only West Germany, Italy and Brazil can better the Uruguayans' two World Cup successes.

As reigning Olympic champions, Uruguay were chosen to host the first

Below: The Uruguay team pose for the camera before their 1950 World Cup match against Brazil.

World Cup finals in 1930, and after progressing with relative ease through their group matches against Romania and Peru, they trounced Yugoslavia 6–1 to reach the final. Bitter rivals Argentina provided the opposition for a match in the new Centenario stadium in Montevideo, a clash of passion and controversy. Disagreements about match balls delayed the kick-off, but the wait was worthwhile and, after trailing 2–1 at half-time, Uruguay came back with goals from Pedro Cea, Iriarte and Hector Castro to win 4–2.

Uruguay, who also claimed five pre-World War II Copa America titles, did not defend their world crown in 1934. In 1950, they took what was arguably their greatest-ever team to the finals in Brazil. The side contained several big names, including Omar Miguez and Victor Andrade, but the great Juan Schiaffino was the real star. The finals of 1950 were organized as a league system, but in the deciding match, the hosts, Brazil, took on the Uruguayans, knowing that a draw would be enough to secure the World Cup. The Brazilians began the match in style and after 48 minutes took the

Above: Uruguay striker Diego Forlan is marked by England's Gary Neville during a 2006 friendly match.

lead, but a goal from the inspirational Schiaffino shook the favourites and, 13 minutes later, Uruguay struck a goal to secure their famous victory.

Uruguay reached the World Cup semi-finals again in 1954 and 1970, but on neither occasion were they able to recapture the success of the past. By 1970, they found themselves struggling to keep pace with their rivals in both the World Cup and the Copa America.

Nevertheless, victory in the 1995 Copa America, runners-up four years later and qualification, after a play-off with Australia, for the 2002 World Cup finals triggered a revival in Uruguayan fortunes. They were unlucky in the World Cup in Japan and South Korea: a refereeing error helped Senegal to a 3–0 lead, and Uruguay's second-half recovery to 3–3 was not enough to avoid elimination. Their qualification for 2010, furthermore, had to be attained through a play-off match against Costa Rica which the South Americans won 2–1 on aggregate. A truly great footballing nation are invited in from the cold as they set their sites on success at the finals in 2010.

France

World Cup Appearances: *12 (1930, 34, 38, 54, 58, 66, 78, 82, 86, 98, 2002, 06)*

World Cup Record: *Winners 1 (1998); runners-up 1 (2006); third place 2 (1958, 86); fourth place 1 (1960)*

How They Qualified: *UEFA play-off winners*

Shirt: *Blue*

The evolution of world football owes a great debt to France – the game's greatest prize was, after all, the brainchild of Frenchman Jules Rimet – so it was fitting that the last World Cup final of the 20th century was won by 'Les Bleus' in Paris. France's only previous international trophy win came at the European Championships of 1984, a competition that had another Frenchman, Henri Delaunay, as its architect.

France's World Cup success of 1998 was memorable not only because it arrived on home soil, but also because it was achieved with a comprehensive 3–0 victory against Brazil, the reigning champions and the tournament's resounding favourites. The man behind this long-awaited triumph was coach Aimé Jacquet, who produced a team that combined an impressive work ethic

Below: Zinedine Zidane, scorer of two goals in the 1998 World Cup final.

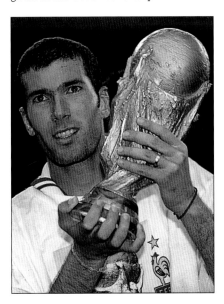

with a high degree of skill. The defensive unit of Fabien Barthez, Lilian Thuram, Laurent Blanc, Marcel Desailly and Bixente Lizarazu was the finest on display at France 1998, and the team's outstanding talent, Zinedine Zidane, ruled the midfield.

Les Bleus' previous best World Cup performances had been their third place in 1958 and 1986. The team of 1986, which lost to West Germany in the semi-finals, still contained many of the players who won the 1984 European Championships under coach Michel Hidalgo. That side is widely regarded as France's greatest-ever line-up, and its strength was the midfield quartet of Luis Fernandez, Jean Tigana, Alain Giresse and Michel Platini. However, just as in 1998, Hidalgo's team lacked an outstanding striker. It was a problem that was finally resolved at Euro 2000. Coach Roger Lemerre retained the 1998 defence and midfield and with the potent attacking quartet of Anelka, Henry, Wiltord and Trezeguet, France justified their billing by cruising through to win the European Championship.

With much the same team as 1998 and 2000, France were favourites for the World

Above: Thierry Henry, France's record highest goalscorer, could be playing in his last World Cup finals.

Cup of 2002, but suffered a shock 1–0 defeat to Senegal in the tournament's curtain-raiser. They went on to finish bottom of the group, without scoring a single goal. Under new coach Jaques Santini, France qualified for the Euro 2004 finals in Portugal, but he resigned after France were beaten by Greece in the quarter-final. Coach Raymond Domenech took France to the final of the 2006 World Cup but the team was defeated by Italy after penalties and the dismissal of the talismanic Zinedine Zidane after a shocking head-butt on Marco Materazzi. At Euro 2008, the team failed to achieve a single point in the group phase, with a 2–0 loss to Italy sealing their fate.

Controversy prevailed on the road to 2010 when Thierry Henry's hand-ball helped set up William Gallas's goal during the play-off, which stopped a spirited Republic of Ireland side from reaching their first World Cup finals since 2002.

Argentina

World Cup Appearances: *14 (1930, 34, 58, 62, 66, 74, 78, 82, 86, 90, 94, 98, 2002, 06)*

World Cup Record: *Winners 2 (1978, 86); runners-up 2 (1930, 90)*

How They Qualified: *Fourth place CONMEBOL*

Shirt: *Blue and white stripes*

If Brazil are the extravagant artists of South American football, then Argentina are the continent's great pragmatists. Twice world champions and 11-time winners of the Copa America, Argentina are one of the most successful teams in post-war international football. At their best, they combine South American flair with rigorous defending and a rare competitive spirit. At their worst, however, they can be cynical, at times with a brutal style of play.

In 1901 Argentina contested South America's first international football match, crossing the River Plate to defeat Uruguay 3–2 in Montevideo. Clashes with Uruguay dominated Argentina's fixture list during the early years of the 20th century, and the two teams also met

Below: Lionel Messi hopes to emulate Maradona's 1986 heroics in South Africa.

in the first ever World Cup finals, held in Uruguay in 1930. Argentina reached the final, which was played before a crowd of 90,000 in Montevideo, after topping their group and beating the USA 6–1 in the semi-final. However, despite the services of the competition's most uncompromising player, Luisito Monti, and tournament top-scorer Guillermo Stabile, Argentina were beaten 4–2.

Forty-eight years after their first World Cup final, Argentina progressed to a second, although this time on home turf against Holland at the Monumental Stadium in Buenos Aires. Valencia striker Mario Kempes proved the hero of the final, scoring twice in a game Argentina eventually won 3–1 after extra time.

For their defence of the world crown in 1982, Argentina were buoyed by the addition of Diego Maradona to their squad. However, the talented 21-year-old was subjected to crude man-marking against both Italy and Brazil, and Argentina crashed out of the competition. Four years later, Maradona, who was by now a match for any close marking, captained his country to victory in the World Cup final against West Germany.

Above: Diego Maradona, Argentina's inspirational skipper, in action at the World Cup finals in 1986.

Argentina and West Germany again contested the final in 1990, but this time the Germans won 1–0 in a final most memorable for the dismissals of Argentines Monzon and Dezotti, who became the first players ever to see a red card in a World Cup final. In 2006 they were eliminated in the quarter-finals after a penalty shoot-out in a bad-tempered game against the hosts Germany.

Diego Maradona returned to the national team in the role of manager at the start of the qualification rounds for the 2010 finals; his unconventional coaching methods and often strange selections, however, left Argentina scraping through and finishing fourth in the CONMEBOL qualification table. Yet with the likes of Lionel Messi pulling the creative strings in midfield, and captained by the combative Javier Mascherano, Argentina will travel to South Africa looking for their third World Cup success in what will be their fifteenth appearence in the competition.

Nigeria

World Cup Appearances: *3 (1994, 98, 2002)*

World Cup Record: *Second round 2 (1994, 98)*

How They Qualified: *Winners CAF Group B*

Shirt: *Green with white trim*

In the 1990s, Nigeria were Africa's leading team, and the most significant threat to the European and South American stranglehold on the World Cup. For many years, African football had been patronized with endless comments about untapped potential, but such encouragement quickly dried up when Nigeria showed just what they could do in the early stages of the French World Cup finals in 1998.

Up until the 1990s, Nigeria's only major footballing success had been victory against Algeria in the final of the 1980 African Nations Cup. The 'Super Eagles' were also runners-up in the Nations Cups in 1984 and 1988, but it was their

Below: Striker Yakubu fights off the challenges of Ghana's Michael Essien.

achievements at junior level that provided the real clues as to what would follow. In 1985 the junior Eagles became the first African team to win the World Under-17 Championships, beating Germany 2–0 in the final. In 1987 and 1989 Nigeria were runners-up in the World Under-17 and Under-19 Championships, and in 1993 they won the Under-17 title for a second time. Among the players who secured success in 1993 were several who became successes in the senior team, notably Nwankwo Kanu, Celestine Babayaro and Wilson Oruma.

In 1994 Nigeria's rapidly ascendant path swept them to a second African Nations Cup victory, and to their first World Cup finals. The Super Eagles made a dramatic start to USA 1994, beating Bulgaria 3–0 and finishing top of their group, which included Argentina. In the second round, the Nigerians were eliminated in extra time by Italy, having led the three-time winners with just a minute of normal time remaining. It proved no more than a minor setback and, although dictator Sani Abacha prevented Nigeria from defending

Above: Nwankwo Kanu was Nigeria's Olympic captain in 1996.

their African Nations Cup in 1996, their momentum was maintained that year with victory against Argentina in the final of the Olympic Games in Atlanta.

Nigeria's progress has not gone unnoticed by scouts from Europe's big clubs, and by the time the Nigerians travelled to their second World Cup finals in France in 1998, Boro Milutinovic's 22-man squad contained just one African-based player. Two years later, the Super Eagles contested the African Nations Cup final on home soil with a team consisting entirely of players based in Europe. Nigeria were defeated by Cameroon on penalties in the 2000 final and finished in third place in 2002, 2004 and 2006. They qualified for the 2002 World Cup finals but finished bottom of a tough group.

Nigeria secured a place at the finals in South Africa in 2010 by finishing top of Group B, which also included Tunisia, Mozambique and Kenya. The team's strong campaign saw them go unbeaten in the third round CAF qualifiers, with three wins and three draws, in what was a fairly open final round of African qualification.

South Korea

World Cup Appearances: *7 (1954, 86, 90, 94, 98, 2002, 06)*

World Cup Record: *Semi-finals 1 (2002)*

How They Qualified: *Winners AFC Group B*

Shirt: *Red*

South Korea are easily Asia's most experienced World Cup campaigners, having appeared at seven World Cup finals – 1954, 1986, 1990, 1994, 1998, 2002 and 2006. Their best appearance came in 2002 when, against all odds, they managed to progress to the semi-finals of the tournament on home soil. On the 25th June 2002, some 65,000 fans attended the semi-final game at the World Cup Stadium in Seoul, South Korea. The contest was against the European powerhouse Germany, and Guus Hiddink's South Korea had already made World Cup history by being the first Asian team to progress to the semi-finals – one better than their neighbour Korea DPR, who reached

the quarter-final in England in 1966. Despite losing the semi-final to a single Michael Ballack strike, South Korea's progress to the last four of a World Cup competition is one of the great achievements in World Cup history.

Since then, South Korea have naturally developed into a real force

Above: South Korea progressed to the semi-finals of the 2006 World Cup.

in both Asian and world football. Currently managed by Huh Jung-Moo, who took over from the unsuccessful Pim Verbeek (now manager of AFC rivals Australia), South Korea progressed to the 2010 finals after finishing top of Group B of the AFC qualifying round, defeating Saudi Arabia and Korea DPR during the campaign.

Captained by the only Korean player to win the UEFA Champions League, Park Ji-Sung (who won the coveted prize with Manchester United in 2008), South Korea will travel to the 2010 finals with high expectations of at least progressing out of their group. The 2010 tournament follows a decent display in Germany four years ago where they won their first World Cup game outside Asia (of course, the previous World Cup was played on home turf in South Korea and Japan), beating Togo 2–1 in Frankfurt. Their spirited campaigns in both 2002 and 2006 bode well for the next World Cup finals, and the mixture of experience in Park Ji-Sung and youth in players such as Lee Chung-Yong suggests South Korea should not be underestimated in South Africa in 2010.

Below: Lee Dong-Gook, one of the all-time greats of South Korean football.

Below: Park Ji-Sung will captain South Korea at the 2010 World Cup finals.

Greece

World Cup Appearances: *1 (1994)*

World Cup Record: *First round 1 (1994)*

How They Qualified: *UEFA play-off winners*

Shirt: *White with blue trim*

Greece is perhaps one of the most inconsistent national football teams of modern times. They have only qualified for one previous World Cup finals – for USA 1994 – and were eliminated in the first round of that tournament. Their record in the European Championships, furthermore, doesn't make for better reading: before 2004, they had qualified only once for the tournament – for Italy 1980 – and were again eliminated in the first round. Despite their inconsistency, however, Greece overturned the odds in the European Championships in 2004 by winning the tournament against the hosts and overwhelming favourites Portugal. It was an outstanding achievement for such an unheralded

Below: Centre-forward Georgios Samaras brings the ball under control.

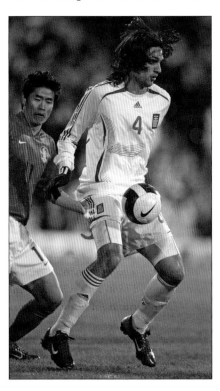

Above: Vassilios Tsiartas threads the ball through midfield.

national football team; the victory in the final in Lisbon was a repeat of the opening fixture when Greece played and beat the hosts and moreover recorded their first-ever win in a major tournament. From that opening game success, Greece went on to beat France in the quarter-finals and the Czech Republic in the semi-finals before beating Portugal again to become the most unlikely of European champions. Playing an ultra-defensive, counter-attacking style, Greece prevailed during the tournament by stifling their opponents' attacks before capitalizing on their own chances in front of goal. Though unpopular, Greece were worthy winners of the tournament, if only for their spirit and organization. It was the zenith of their international status, however, and they have since failed to replicate such form.

Their qualification for a place in the finals in South Africa began in UEFA Group 2, alongside Latvia, Israel and Switzerland as well as Luxembourg and Moldova. It was a tight affair and Greece managed to book a place in the play-offs, largely due to the ten goals from Europe's top goalscorer Theofanis

Gekas. In the play-offs, they were drawn against Ukraine and they booked their place in the 2010 tournament by beating the 'Yellow-Blues' 1–0 on their home soil in Donetsk.

Greece will travel to South Africa with a view to progressing from their group. Though numerous players from the 2004 European Championship winning squad have since retired, a few experienced heads remain to guide the squad through the inevitable intensities of a World Cup campaign: midfielder Kostas Katsouranis and centre-forward Angelos Charisteas both played during that victorious evening in Lisbon in 2004, and many younger players such as Georgios Samaras and Alexandros Tziolis will look to emulate their predecessors and buck the odds at the tournament in South Africa. Perhaps most importantly for the Greece team, the Euro 2004-winning coach Otto Rehhagel remains in the managerial hotseat and will again guide the team in their latest quest for international football glory.

England

World Cup Appearances: *12 (1950, 54, 58, 62, 66, 70, 82, 86, 90, 98, 2002, 06)*

World Cup Record: *Winners 1 (1966); fourth place 1 (1990)*

How They Qualified: *Winners UEFA Group 6*

Shirt: *White*

England has a special place in football's history; it is the birthplace of the game, and the site of the world's most famous domestic competition, the FA Cup. England also played in the first recorded international match, drawing 0–0 with Scotland in 1872.

In the early years of international football, England competed exclusively against Wales, Scotland and Ireland, and it was not until 1908 that 'foreign' opposition was encountered in the shape of Austria. England beat the Austrians 6–1, and later that year recorded victories against Hungary (7–0) and Bohemia (4–0). Confidence soon grew – probably beyond ability – and by the inter-war period England were convinced that they

Below: Wayne Rooney will hope to be on top form for South Africa 2010.

Above: Glen Johnson's qualifying performances should see him in the team for his first World Cup in 2010.

were the greatest team in the world. They did not get the chance to prove it because of a dispute with FIFA over payments for amateur players, which meant they did not participate in the early World Cup finals during the 1930s.

Under manager Walter Winterbottom, England made their World Cup debut in Brazil in 1950. It was a disastrous experience, with the team suffering the indignity of a defeat by the USA and elimination at the first hurdle. Worse followed when, in 1953, England were beaten 6–3 by Hungary at Wembley. Another poor World Cup campaign in 1962 proved too much for Walter Winterbottom, and he was replaced by Ipswich Town boss Alf Ramsey.

The pragmatic Ramsey made better use of the talented players available, and on home soil in 1966 the famous 'Wingless Wonders' claimed the nation's only World Cup success to date. The 4–2 win over West Germany, in which striker Geoff Hurst scored a hat-trick, remains the most celebrated game in England's footballing history.

Ramsey and his team, which was led by Bobby Moore and built around the abundantly talented Bobby Charlton,

attempted to repeat the trick in Mexico four years later, but were beaten by West Germany in the quarter-finals. England entered a steady decline in the 1970s, and when the team failed to qualify for the 1974 World Cup finals, Ramsey retired. Only Bobby Robson managed to approach Ramsey's achievement, with England going out on penalties to Germany in the 1990 World Cup semi-final and finishing in fourth place.

Sven-Göran Eriksson, England's first foreign manager, took over in 2001 and lead the side to the last eight of the 2002 tournament where they lost to eventual winners Brazil. He did the same in 2006 in Germany, where the Three Lions lost to Portugal on penalties in the quarter-final.

Following a brief and unsuccessful spell under Steve McLaren, England were taken over by Fabio Capello, who lost only one game during qualifying for the 2010 finals. Bringing a more disciplined and pragmatic attitude and building his team around the talented Wayne Rooney, the Italian will expect his players to progress to the later stages of the finals in South Africa.

Below: Frank Lampard, who played in every game at the 2006 World Cup.

USA

World Cup Appearances: *8 (1930, 34, 50, 90, 94, 98, 2002, 06)*

World Cup Record: *Third place 1 (1930)*

How They Qualified: *Winners CONCACAF*

Shirt: *White*

Association football has struggled to establish itself in the United States, where the gridiron game remains infinitely more popular. It would, however, be wrong to ignore the colourful history of the USA 'soccer' team, which has achieved several impressive victories since 1990, enhanced, no doubt, by the establishment of the professional Major League Soccer in 1996.

The United States made its first significant impression upon the world game in 1930, when it was among the 13 nations to send a team to the inaugural World Cup finals in Uruguay. The USA team included six former British professionals and progressed to the last four of the competition, with victories over Belgium and Paraguay. But the

Below: Landon Donovan celebrates scoring with his team-mates.

fairytale came to an end in the semi-finals where they were crushed 6–1 by eventual runners-up Argentina. Four years later they were back in the finals, but this time the crushing defeat came in the first round, with Italy dishing out a 7–1 beating.

Until 2002, the USA's greatest World Cup achievement came at the finals in 1950. A group match against a highly fancied England team that was unbeaten since World War II seemed to offer little hope for a team of American part-timers. However, on a bumpy pitch in Belo Horizonte, Brazil, England conceded the game's only goal to Larry Gaetjens. USA 1 England 0 remains one of the biggest shock results in footballing history.

In the 1970s, United States football looked to be on the verge of a new era, with the expensively set-up North American Soccer League seeming to offer the sport a long-awaited lifeline. But the treatment proved ineffective and the league collapsed. Twenty years later the new era finally arrived when the USA qualified for Italia 1990, their first World Cup finals for 40 years. Results were a disappointment in Italy, with Bob Gansler's

Above: Midfielder Benny Feilhaber is playing at his first World Cup in 2010.

team losing all three of their games. In 1991 a new coach, Yugoslav Bora Milutinovic, was chosen to lead the USA into the 1994 finals on home turf. Milutinovic expertly blended youth, in the shape of Alexi Lalas and Cobi Jones, with experienced players such as Thomas Dooley and John Harkes, and the hosts gave an impressive account of themselves. The USA qualified through their group after a draw with Switzerland and a 2–1 win against Colombia, but went down 1–0 to eventual champions Brazil in the second round.

After losing all their games in the World Cup finals of 1998, the USA surprised the world in 2002. Under coach Bruce Arena, they qualified from the group stage, beating Portugal, then beat Mexico 2–0 before going out in the quarter-finals 1–0 to Germany. They failed to build on that success in the next World Cup finals, however, losing all their games and exiting in the group stages in Germany in 2006.

The USA qualified for the 2010 competition in October 2009 following a 3–2 away win against Honduras. Coached by Bob Bradley and captained by Carlos Bocanegra, the team are fast becoming a true force in world football.

Algeria

World Cup Appearances: *2 (1982, 86)*

World Cup Record: *First round 2 (1982, 86)*

How They Qualified: *Winners CAF Group C*

Shirt: *White with green trim*

Algeria have qualified for the World Cup finals three times since they first entered in 1966 (when they subsequently withdrew). Their first appearance came in Spain in 1982 when they were drawn in Group 2 with West Germany, Austria and Chile. It was a very tight group and Algeria missed out on a place in the second round only on goal difference; after causing an upset in their opening fixture against West Germany – beating the hosts 2–1 following goals from Rabah Madjer and Lakhdar Belloumi (respectively the second and third highest goalscorers in Algeria's international history) – and beating Chile in their final group game, Algeria had to settle for third place in the group, narrowly missing out on a spot in the next round on goal difference.

Four years later, in Mexico in 1986, 'Les Fennecs' (The Desert Foxes) were drawn in a tough group that featured Northern Ireland, Spain and Brazil. The north Africans finished bottom of their group, losing to both Brazil and Spain and salvaging a draw against Northern Ireland.

Despite not qualifying for a World Cup again for some 24 years, Algeria managed to maintain success on the continent: they hosted the African Nations Cup in 1990 and won the competition for the first time, beating Nigeria 1-0 in front of 200,000 fans in Algiers.

Algeria qualified for the 2010 World Cup finals after finishing as joint winners of Group C of the CAF qualification process. Topping their group with identical records to bitter rivals Egypt – they both won four, drew one, lost one, scored nine and conceded four – Algeria were forced to meet their neighbours again in a tie-break contest held at a neutral venue in north Africa. The play-off was a tumultuous affair: taking place in Sudan in November 2009, the match ended 1–0 to Algeria following a goal by Antar Yahia, yet the contest was marred by crowd trouble in both the Algerian and Egyptian capitals. Nevertheless, Algeria will travel to South Africa dreaming of progressing further than their predecessors in 1982 and 1986. Coached by Rabah Saadane, who also led the team to the finals of the 1986 World Cup, Algeria boast the attacking experience of Rafik Saifi, who has scored 18 goals in 55 caps for Les Fennecs. They are captained by midfield stalwart Yazid Mansouri, who plays alongside Wolfsburg midfielder Karim Ziani in the middle of the park. With a decent mixture of experienced heads and young talent, Algeria will hope to progress beyond the group stage at the finals in South Africa in 2010.

Below: Algeria line up for the African Cup of Nations final in 1990.

Slovenia

World Cup Appearances: *1 (2002)*
World Cup Record: *First round 1 (2002)*
How They Qualified: *UEFA play-off winners*
Shirt: *White with green trim*

Slovenia were one of the extraordinary success stories of the 2010 World Cup qualification rounds. They reached only their second World Cup finals by beating Russia in their play-off match and heading through on the away goals rule; it was an amazing achievement for the former Yugoslav republic better known for skiing.

Their 2010 qualification campaign mirrored Slovenia's previous World Cup qualification success, when they beat Romania in the play-offs to reach the 2002 World Cup finals in Japan and South Korea. The man who took much of the credit for Slovenia's qualification in 2002 was arguably Slovenia's best-ever player, Srecko Katanec.

Katanec became coach of the newly independent Slovenia in November 1998, and he affected a remarkable turnaround in their fortunes. Slovenia had gained just one point in their qualifying matches for

the 1998 World Cup, yet under Katanec they qualified for the 2000 European Championship in Holland and Belgium after beating the Ukraine in their play-off.

Slovenia gave a good account of themselves at the 2000 European Championship finals, drawing 3–3 with

Above: Joy for captain Zlatko Zahovic as Slovenia qualify for the 2002 finals.

their neighbours Yugoslavia and proving themselves to be far from the pushovers they were expected to be.

Their quest for international recognition culminated with a respectable World Cup qualifying campaign in 2002 and subsequent qualification via the play-offs. They were knocked out of the finals, however, without scoring a solitary point. Slovenia have since continued their qualifying success on the international scene and escaped a group containing seasoned competitors Slovakia and the Czech Republic to book their place in the 2010 finals at Russia's surprise expense. They travel to South Africa as outsiders and many will expect them to crash out in the group stages. It remains to be seen whether coach Matjaz Kek has any further surprises up his sleeve.

Far left: Marko Suler made his first appearance for Slovenia in 2008.

Left: Defender Bojan Jokic fights off England's Glen Johnson.

Germany

World Cup Appearances: *16 (1934, 38, 54, 58, 62, 66, 70, 74, 78, 82, 86, 90, 94, 98, 2002, 06)*

World Cup Record: *winners 3 (1954, 74, 90); runners-up 4 (1966, 82, 86, 2002); third place 3 (1934, 70, 2006); fourth place 1 (1958)*

How They Qualified: *Winners UEFA Group 4*

Shirt: *White with black trim*

Note: Records for 1950–91 are for West Germany

Despite the protestations of English and Italian fans, Germany are Europe's most successful football team. Seven appearances in the final of a World Cup, including three victories, and three successes in the European Championships, provide irrefutable evidence of their superiority.

Prior to World War II, Germany's record was modest, with third place at the 1934 World Cup tournament being the pinnacle of their achievements. However, after the war, the country was divided and the western half quickly developed into a football superpower. In 1950, West Germany joined FIFA, and four years

Below: Michael Ballack, Germany's captain and midfield playmaker.

later they won their first World Cup with a shock 3–2 victory against the tournament favourites, Hungary, who had beaten West Germany 8–3 in the group phase. In England, 12 years later, West Germany were back in the World Cup final. Having clawed themselves back into the match against the hosts with a last-minute equalizer from Wolfgang Weber, the Germans fell victim to Geoff Hurst's controversial goal and England won the match 4–2.

For West Germany the defeat was tempered by the emergence of sweeper Franz Beckenbauer, who became the single most important figure in German football. In the 1970s, Beckenbauer became the kingpin in West Germany's greatest team, playing alongside fellow legends Sepp Maier, Paul Breitner and Gerd Müller. It was a line-up that swept all before them, clinching first the European Championship of 1972 and then the World Cup two years later.

In the 1980s, Beckenbauer returned to national team duty as coach, and led the side to the 1986 World Cup final. Four years later, 'der Kaiser' went one better, guiding his team, which was built around key players Jürgen Kohler, Lothar Matthäus and Jürgen Klinsmann, to

Above: Beckenbauer acknowledges the crowd after World Cup victory in 1974.

victory against Argentina in the final of Italia 1990. In 1996, a united Germany, captained by Klinsmann, claimed its first major trophy with victory over the Czech Republic in the final of Euro 1996 at Wembley. This proved to be their last noteworthy impression at a finals in the 20th century.

Germany qualified for the 2002 World Cup finals only after a play-off, but surprisingly, with what was regarded as one of their poorest teams, they managed to get through to the final itself. Under coach Rudi Voller, they tested Brazil before losing 2–0. They exited Euro 2004 without winning a game, but under new coach Jürgen Klinsmann they reached the World Cup semi-finals in 2006, conceding two extra-time goals to Italy.

In the latter half of the 2000s, Germany reached the final of Euro 2008, but a fine first-half goal from Spain's Fernando Torres was the only goal of the game. The road to 2010 was a relatively straightforward one, with Germany winning eight and losing only two of their games in Group 4. They return to the World's premier footballing stage looking to reach their eighth final and claim their fourth World Cup.

Australia

World Cup Appearances: *2 (1974, 2006)*

World Cup Record: *Second round 1 (2006)*

How They Qualified: *Winners AFC Group A*

Shirt: *Yellow with green trim*

Despite the lack of on-field success, soccer in Australia has been making steady progress since the 1960s. The decade began in controversy, when the Australian Soccer Football Association was found guilty of poaching Austrian players, and the ASFA was banned by FIFA for three years. Fortunately, the Australian Soccer Federation emerged to overthrow the ASFA in 1961. Two years later Australia was welcomed back by FIFA.

After missing out on qualification for the 1970 World Cup finals in Mexico, the 'Socceroos' earned a place at the subsequent finals in Germany in 1974. The Australians won just one point from their three games, thanks to a goalless draw with Chile, but their achievements had been sufficient to stir interest back home. In 1977, a 14-team national league was formed, and with 350,000 registered junior players the future was looking brighter for Australian soccer.

The mini-boom of the late 1970s, however, failed to develop into anything more significant, and it was not until the mid-1990s that the Socceroos again knocked cricket off the back pages of the national papers. In 1993, Australia narrowly missed

Above: Harry Kewell is one of Australia's most experienced players.

qualifying for the World Cup finals in the United States when they lost 2–1 on aggregate in a play-off against Argentina. Four years later, a Socceroos team led by former England coach Terry Venables suffered a similar heartache, surrendering a 2–0 lead in the second leg of the France 1998 play-off against Iran.

The disappointment continued in 2002 when the Socceroos squandered a first-leg advantage, losing 3–0 to Uruguay in Monteviedo. Under new coach Guus Huddink, however, they surprised many in 2006 by successfully negotiating their way into the second round of the World Cup in Germany, only to lose in the knockout stage to Italy's stoppage-time penalty.

Australia competed for the first time against teams from the AFC confederation in the qualification for the 2010 World Cup finals. They finished top of Group A, ahead of Japan by five points, and head into the finals as spirited underdogs.

Left: Tim Cahill holds the ball aloft as Australia celebrate a win over Croatia.

Serbia

World Cup Appearances: *As Yugoslavia 8 (1930, 50, 54, 58, 62, 74, 82, 90); as Serbia and Montenegro 2 (1998, 2006)*

World Cup Record: *Semi-finals 1 (1930)*

How They Qualified: *Winners UEFA Group 7*

Shirt: *Red*

The Serbian international football team have a colourful World Cup history, not least appearing in the first-ever tournament in Uruguay in 1930 and progressing to the semi-finals, where they met the hosts. This magnificent achievement came under their previous moniker Yugoslavia, and it wasn't matched until some 30 years later when they progressed to the same stage in Chile in 1962. That year they lost 3–1 to Czechoslovakia, who went on to lose by the same score to Brazil in the final.

Yugoslavia entered the World Cup wilderness in subsequent years and didn't qualify for the competition again until West Germany 1974. Drawn alongside Scotland, Zaire and Brazil, Yugoslavia finished top of their group and progressed to the second round. It wasn't to be, however, as Yugoslavia exited the tournament bottom of the second round group after failing to win another game at the tournament. Their next trip to a World Cup finals occurred in Spain in 1982 when they failed to progress beyond the group stages. Their campaign at Italia 1990 proved much more fruitful, however, and Yugoslavia progressed to the quarter-finals, where they were knocked out by Argentina on penalties.

The national team was renamed Serbia and Montenegro in February 2003 following the break-up of Yugoslavia; the renamed side quickly garnered a great defensive reputation following their qualification campaign for the 2006 World Cup finals which saw one goal conceded in ten games. This fantastic work was quickly undone, however, when they lost every game in the finals in Germany and exited once again at the group stages.

Serbia entered the 2010 qualifying campaign as an independent nation and quickly secured their place in South Africa, finishing first ahead of group favourites France and again conceding the least amount of goals in the group. The 2010 team has a vast array of footballing talent which includes the team captain Dejan Stankovic, the combative defender Nemanja Vidic and the tall, accomplished forward Nikola Zigic. The Serbian team will head to South Africa 2010 with strong expectations of reaching the knockout stages.

Below: Milos Krasic shrugs off the challenge of France's Patrice Evra.

Ghana

World Cup Appearances: *1 (2006)*
World Cup Record: *Second round 1 (2006)*
How They Qualified: *Winners CAF Group D*
Shirt: *White with black trim*

Despite their World Cup infancy – a first appearance came in Germany in 2006 – Ghana is one of Africa's most successful international sides. The west Africans have won the African Cup of Nations four times: in 1963, 1965, 1978 and 1982 and trail only Egypt in overall victories in the continental competition. They also came close to regaining the title in 2008, hosting the event and finishing third overall.

It therefore came as no surprise to see Ghana qualify as the first African team for the 2010 World Cup (excluding, of course, the hosts South Africa, who qualified automatically), topping CAF Group D and securing their place at the tournament in September 2009. The 'Black Stars' will expect to eclipse their previous World Cup performance, where they managed to be the only African team to escape their group, which included seasoned World Cup teams such as Italy and the USA. However, the quarter-final

Above: John Mensah controls the ball during qualification for South Africa 2010.

Below: Michael Essien tracks the ball in the heart of the Ghana midfield.

draw was a difficult one for the Black Stars, as they met four-time World Champions Brazil. The contest was over after five minutes when World Cup legend Ronaldo – playing in his third finals – scored a record-breaking fifteenth World Cup goal, surpassing Gerd Müller's total of 14 set in the early 1970s. The landmark goal proved too much for the Ghanaians and, despite a spirited first half, they eventually capitulated to a 3–0 loss. Despite the humbling defeat to the South American powerhouse, Ghana left the competition with an enhanced reputation and a growing respect from international teams outside the African continent.

The road to South Africa 2010 was relatively straightforward for Ghana: following a third-place finish in the African Nations Cup in 2008 (having lost

to beaten finalists Cameroon), the Black Stars moved as high as number 25 in FIFA's international rankings. Drawn alongside Benin, Mali and Sudan, Ghana finished top of Group D in the third round of the CAF qualification process – losing a single match against Benin only after they qualified – and thus guaranteed a safe passage to both the 2010 African Cup of Nations and the 2010 World Cup.

Captained by the combative Stephen Appiah and boasting experienced midfielders such as Michael Essien and Sulley Ali Muntari, Ghana are one of the strongest sides on the African continent and will hope to progress into the knockout stages in South Africa.

Holland

World Cup Appearances: *8 (1934, 38, 74, 78, 90, 94, 98, 2006)*

World Cup Record: *Runners-up 2 (1974, 78); fourth place 1 (1998)*

How They Qualified: *Winners UEFA Group 9*

Shirt: *Orange*

Few international teams have been more deserving of the adjective 'great' than the Dutch team of the 1970s. Although they did not win the World Cup, the team of Johan Cruyff, Rudi Krol and Arie Haan illuminated the modern game in a way that perhaps only Brazil have managed before. Holland, coached by former Ajax boss and the godfather of 'total football' Rinus Michels, played with a fluency that made his team a favourite with neutrals and football purists alike.

In 1974, Holland qualified for their first World Cup finals for 36 years, having competed without success at both the 1934 and 1938 finals. The Dutch breezed through the first qualifying group before producing an outstanding display to beat reigning champions Brazil in the second

Below: Marco Van Basten and Ruud Gullit, Holland's heroes of Euro 1988.

phase and book their place in the final against hosts West Germany.

Holland began the 1974 final in dramatic fashion, Neeskens scoring from the penalty spot after Cruyff had been brought down in the first minute. The Dutch dominated the opening phase of the game but failed to find a second goal and, after 25 minutes, the Germans struck an equalizer with a penalty of their own. A second-half goal from Gerd Müller clinched the game for the hosts.

The Dutch, minus Cruyff, who had retired from international football, were back in the World Cup final four years later, but once more they came unstuck against a host nation, this time Argentina. It proved the swansong for the total football team, and it was not until a new generation of stars emerged in the late 1980s that Holland again found themselves fighting for major honours. The European Championships of 1988 saw the second great Dutch team, including Marco Van Basten, Frank Rijkaard, Ronald Koeman and Ruud Gullit, win the competition with a 2–0 victory against the USSR in Munich. Several Dutch teams have subsequently flirted with success, most notably Guus

Above: The talented Arjen Robben is a key member of the Dutch national side.

Hiddink's side that finished fourth in France in 1998, but all too often internal disputes over tactics, money and managers undermine attempts to recapture the glory days of the 1970s.

Heading into the 2000s, Holland failed to qualify for the first World Cup of the new millenium following a poor campaign under manager Louis van Gaal. They reached the subsequent European Championships in 2004, however, but were eliminated in the semi-final by hosts Portugal in a 2–1 defeat. Two years later, at the World Cup finals in Germany, Holland were drawn in the 'group of death' with Argentina, the Ivory Coast and Serbia and Montenegro. The Dutch reached the first round of the knockout stages but were again eliminated by Portugal in a tumultuous match that saw four players – two from each side – sent off.

One of the first UEFA teams to qualify for the 2010 finals, Holland travel to South Africa as a firm favourite, and with attacking talent including the likes of Robin van Persie and Wesley Sneijder, they will hope to emulate the glory days of the great 'Oranje'.

Denmark

World Cup Appearances: *3 (1986, 98, 2002)*
World Cup Record: *Quarter-finals 1 (1998); second round 2 (1986, 2002)*
How They Qualified: *Winners UEFA Group 1*
Shirt: *Red*

In 1992 Denmark gatecrashed the European Championships and won a competition for which they had failed to qualify, completing one of the most compelling tales in the history of international football. The Danes had finished as runners-up to Yugoslavia in their qualifying group for Euro 1992, but, with the Balkans on the verge of vicious conflict, Yugoslavia withdrew and Denmark received a late pass into the tournament.

Goals from Larsen and Elstrup were enough to overcome a highly fancied French team in the quarter-finals, and

Below: John Jensen celebrates scoring against Germany in the final of Euro 1992.

set up a match against the even more promising Dutch side in the semi-final. It seemed that Holland, with the likes of Bergkamp, Van Basten, Koeman, Rijkaard, Gullit and Van Tiggelen in their line-up, could not fail to win, but the Danes were on top of their game and they never fell behind in a match that ended 2–2 after extra time. Denmark won the penalty shoot-out following a miss from Marco Van Basten, and the Danes were now the neutrals' favourite against Germany in the final. The fairytale came true with goals from John Jensen and Kim Vilfort in a 2–0 victory.

Ironically, Denmark's triumph at Euro 1992 was achieved without the country's greatest player, Michael Laudrup, who was in dispute with Moller Nielson over tactics. Laudrup had been Denmark's star at the 1986 World Cup finals, playing a key role in the 2–0 victory over West Germany and in the 6–1 thrashing of Uruguay. The appointment of Swedish coach

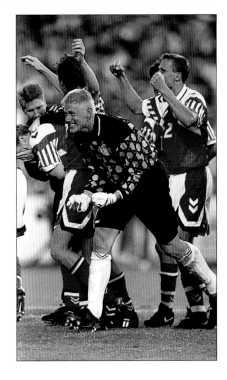

Above: Peter Schmeichel and team-mates enjoy their victory at Euro 1992.

Bo Johansson, following a poor showing at Euro 1996, meant Michael Laudrup returned to the fold.

With their star player back, alongside brother Brian, Denmark did well at the 1998 World Cup finals, losing in the quarter-finals 3–2 to tournament runners-up Brazil. Without the Laudrups – both of whom retired in 1999 – Denmark managed to reach the knockout stages of the 2002 World Cup, where they lost to England 3–0.

Following their failure to qualify for the 2006 finals, Denmark entered Group 1 of the 2010 qualifying campaign alongside talented teams such as Sweden and Portugal. The Danes booked their place in the tournament by finishing first in the group, forcing Portugal into the play-offs. With the experience of Christian Poulsen and the youthful industry of players such as Nicklas Bendtner – who won Danish Footballer of the Year in 2009 – Denmark will relish the opportunity to revive the glory days of 1992 in South Africa 18 years later.

Japan

World Cup Appearances: *3 (1994, 2002, 06)*

World Cup Record: *Second round 1 (2002)*

How They Qualified: *Second AFC Group 2*

Shirt: *Blue*

Although not yet a significant force in world football, Japan has made great strides in recent years and now has the fan base, not to mention the financial clout, to become Asia's dominant footballing nation. Japan and South Korea, the co-hosts of the 2002 World Cup, both exceeded expectations and went a long way towards joining the football 'establishment'.

The formation of the professional J-League in 1993 was a key factor in FIFA's decision to grant the Japanese and Koreans the first World Cup of the new millennium. The J-League proved an immediate success, attracting huge crowds and a host of foreign stars, among them England's Gary Lineker, Brazil's Dunga and Italy's Salvatore Schillaci. The formation of the J-League also coincided with an upturn in the fortunes of Japan's national team,

Below: Shunsuke Nakamura is a key member of the 2010 World Cup team.

although after winning the 1992 Asian Cup they failed to qualify for the 1994 World Cup finals.

Japan put the disappointment of 1994 behind them, and four years later, under the guidance of popular coach Takeshi Okada, they qualified for their first World Cup finals. However, France 1998 proved a disappointment for the team, and defeats in their three games illustrated how much work still needed to be done. One positive aspect of the finals was the emergence of 21-year-old midfielder Hidetoshi Nakata, who moved to Italian Serie A-side Perugia in 1998. Nakata was an instant hit in Italy and, after only one full season, the then-reigning Asian Footballer of the Year was transferred to AS Roma, then Parma, in multimillion-dollar deals.

At the World Cup 2002 they surpassed themselves, topping their group with a notable win against Russia, before losing 1–0 in the second round to Turkey. Players such as Nakata, Morioka, Junichi Inamoto and Shinji Ono (in the 2002 UEFA Cup-winning Feyenoord side) made themselves known to a worldwide TV audience. They qualified again for the

Above: Japan line up for a friendly game against Brazil prior to the 2006 World Cup.

2006 World Cup, but defeats by Brazil and Australia, and a draw against Croatia, led to their early exit.

Japan were the second team to qualify for the tournament in South Africa in 2010. After the hosts, Japan booked their place in the tournament with a 1–0 win over Uzbekistan in June 2008. They finished second to Australia in Group A of the Asian qualifying round, winning four, drawing three and losing only one game during the campaign. With the experience of Shunsuke Nakamura patrolling the midfield and the invention of seasoned J-League players such as Shinji Okazaki and Keiji Tamada leading the attack, Japan will enter the 2010 finals with high expectations and strong hopes of going one better than their record of the first knockout stage. Their surprise progression as host nation in 2002 led to a greater consistency within the Japanese national team, and their opponents will view the current team as a serious threat during the finals in South Africa in 2010.

Cameroon

World Cup Appearances: *5 (1982, 90, 94, 98, 2002)*

World Cup Record: *Quarter-finals 1 (1990)*

How They Qualified: *Winners CAF Group A*

Shirt: *Green*

In the 1980s the 'Indomitable Lions' of Cameroon became the leading lights of African football, reaching three consecutive finals in the African Nations Cup, and qualifying for the 1982 World Cup finals in Spain. The Cameroon Football Federation only joined FIFA in 1962, but by the end of the 1990s the Lions had established themselves as a genuine force within the game.

Centre-forward Roger Milla was the pivotal figure in Cameroon's ascendancy of the 1980s and 1990s. Milla, who was voted African Footballer of the Century, was a

Below: Cameroon's indomitable striker Roger Milla at Italia 1990.

youthful 30-year-old when he played in his and Cameroon's first World Cup finals in Spain in 1982. Under Yugoslav coach Branko Zutic, the Africans played with great discipline in their group games, and drew all three of their matches, conceding their only goal in the 1–1 draw with eventual champions Italy.

Cameroon's reputation as an emerging footballing power was confirmed by victory in the 1984 African Nations Cup final, and only a defeat on penalties against Egypt prevented them from retaining their African crown in 1986. A trilogy of consecutive finals was completed with victory over Nigeria in 1988, and the Lions travelled to the World Cup in Italy in 1990 as the continental champions. Cameroon kicked-off the tournament against World Cup holders Argentina and exceeded expectations by winning 1–0, despite having two players sent off. A 2–0 win against Romania in the next game had 38-year-old double-goalscorer Roger Milla dancing around the corner flag.

Above: Samuel Eto'o is a formidable member of the Cameroon attack.

Colombia were Cameroon's next opponents and Milla was again the hero, scoring both goals in a 2–1 victory. England brought the fairytale to an end in the quarter-finals, although Bobby Robson's team needed a penalty in extra time to seal the victory.

Cameroon qualified for the World Cup finals of 1994, 1998 and 2002, but could not emulate their success of Italia 1990. However, they won the Olympic Games title in 2002, beating Spain in the final, and with players such as Rigobert Song and Samuel Eto'o they won the African Nations Cup in 2000 and 2002, and were runners-up in 2008.

Qualification to the 2010 finals in South Africa was secured after finishing top of Group A of CAF. Despite a slow start, Cameroon ensured their place at the finals after beating Morocco in Fez. They travel to South Africa hoping to draw upon the spirit of Italia 1990, and with midfielders such as Alexandre Song shielding their defence, Cameroon will fancy their chances of getting past the group stage.

Italy

World Cup Appearances: *16 (1934, 38, 50, 54, 62, 66, 70, 74, 78, 82, 86, 90, 94, 98, 2002, 06)*

World Cup Record: *Winners 4 (1934, 38, 82, 2006); runners-up 2 (1970, 94); third place 1 (1990); fourth place 1 (1978)*

How They Qualified: *Winners UEFA Group 8*

Shirt: *Blue*

Italy were the first European team to win the World Cup, and having won the trophy on three further occasions, they regard themselves as the continent's pre-eminent footballing nation.

Italy enjoyed its first taste of glory at the 1934 World Cup, winning the Jules Rimet trophy on home soil, with a team coached by Vittorio Pozzo and which included three Argentines, Pozzo led Italy to a second World Cup success four years later in France, but this time the South American exiles had been replaced by Italian-born talent.

Italy's domination of world football was brought to an abrupt end by the outbreak of war in 1939, and it was not until 1950 that the 'Azzurri' (Blues) were given the opportunity to defend their title. Sadly, the Superga aircrash of 1949, which had

Below: Paolo Rossi scores in a 3–2 victory over Brazil in the 1982 World Cup.

wiped out the successful Torino team of the 1940s, left the national team without many of its first-choice players, and the dream of a hat-trick of World Cups ended with elimination at the group phase.

In 1968, an Italian team that included Dino Zoff, Sandro Mazzola, Giacinto Facchetti and Gigi Riva won the European Championships, beating Yugoslavia 2–0 in Rome. With the exception of Zoff, these players would also help Italy to the World Cup final in Mexico two years later. The Italians, however, met arguably the greatest team in the history of the game in the shape of Brazil, and were beaten 4–1.

In 1982, Italy finally added to the two titles they had won in the 1930s. The Spanish finals in 1982 began quietly for Italy, and they drew their opening three matches before finding form with victories against Brazil and Argentina. In the semi-final, controversial striker Paolo Rossi proved the hero, scoring both goals in a 2–0 victory against Poland to book the Italians' place in the final. Rossi struck again in the final against West Germany, and further goals from Marco Tardelli and Alessandro Altobelli secured a 3–1 victory. A record fourth World Cup was almost added at USA 1994, but Italy were defeated in a penalty shoot-out against Brazil.

Above: Fabio Cannavaro, the Azzurri's most capped player and captain.

After being within seconds of winning the European Championship in 2000 (France won with a 'golden goal'), Italian hopes were high for the World Cup in 2002. But Italy lost again to a golden goal, this time in the second round against co-hosts South Korea.

A determined Italy entered the 2006 World Cup finals following damning allegations of match fixing within the Italian domestic league. The national team performed splendidly, however, winning their fourth final against old rivals France on penalties after a 1–1 draw in Berlin.

Once again under the tutelage of World Cup-winning manager Marcello Lippi – following an unsuccessful tenure under Roberto Donadoni – Italy enter the 2010 finals looking to defend their crown for the first time since their last success in the competition in 1982.

Paraguay

World Cup Appearances: *7 (1930, 50, 58, 86, 98, 2002, 06)*

World Cup Record: *Second round 3 (1986, 98, 2002)*

How They Qualified: *Third place CONMEBOL*

Shirt: *Red and white stripes*

Paraguay are a rising force in South American football, and they reached the 2010 World Cup finals with a confident qualifying campaign. Traditionally one of the poorer footballing nations of South America, Paraguay has only a semi-professional league. This has forced the country's leading players to move abroad to earn more money, but the experience they have gained at club level has also benefited the national side.

Paraguay will be playing in their eighth World Cup finals in South Africa and it will be their fourth successive appearance in the finals. During France 1998, Paraguay recorded perhaps their best achievement yet in a World Cup tournament by reaching the second round for only the second time in their history. They took hosts and eventual winners France to extra time before falling to the first 'golden goal' in a World Cup finals, scored by France's Laurent Blanc. Paraguay defended heroically against France, garnering noteworthy performances from

Above: Carlos Gamarra, one of the best defenders in South American football.

veteran goalkeeper Jose Luis Chilavert, and centre-back Carlos Gamarra, who also won CONMEBOL's Best Defender of the Year in 1998.

Four years later in Japan and South Korea, Paraguay again reached the last 16, having escaped a group featuring South Africa, Slovenia and Spain. Again they were defeated in the first knockout stage,

Above: Paraguay's legendary goalkeeper Jose Luis Chilavert.

this time losing 1–0 to the eventual finalists Germany.

Their third successive World Cup finals tournament, however, was one to forget. Drawn alongside Sweden, England and Trinidad and Tobago, Paraguay lost their opening two fixtures and could only finish third in their group after beating Trinidad and Tobago in the final group game. Following their exit from the tournament, the side entered a state of transition with Paraguayan stalwarts Carlos Gamarra and Celso Ayala retiring from the international scene. It was around this time, however, that a new crop of players began to emerge: attackers such as Roque Santa Cruz and Nelson Valdez were making big impressions in European leagues.

Paraguay head to South Africa with a strong qualifying record (indeed they qualified before Argentina), but it remains to be seen whether they can consolidate their consistency over four weeks of intense tournament football.

Left: The Paraguay team line up for a match against Wales in 2006.

New Zealand

World Cup Appearances: *1 (1982)*
World Cup Record: *First round 1 (1982)*
How They Qualified: *Winners OFC qualification group; won play-off against 5th AFC team*
Shirt: *White*

Since Australia moved to the AFC qualification group at the start of the 2010 World Cup qualifying campaign, the tournament berths for the Oceania qualification group (OFC) were reduced to 0.5, which meant the top-placed team at the end of the rounds faced a tough play-off against the fifth-placed team in the AFC group. New Zealand – the only remaining seeded team in the OFC confederation – progressed relatively easily from the OFC group, which featured New Caledonia, Fiji and Vanuata, none of whom has come close to qualifying for the World Cup before. The 'All Whites' won five games and lost only to Fiji during the campaign (having already progressed to the World Cup finals). Their play-off against fifth-placed AFC team Bahrain, furthermore, was a nervy affair, but New Zealand booked their place in the World Cup finals for only the second time in their history after a 1–0 aggregate win over two legs.

The only other occasion the All Whites progressed to the finals of a World Cup came in Spain in 1982 when they were entered into Group 6 with the USSR, Scotland and international powerhouse Brazil. They lost all three games, conceding 12 goals and scoring only twice in the process, and finished bottom of their group. They salvaged some international respect, however, for their spirited display against Scotland in their opening fixture in Malaga: the Scots, leading 3–0, were pegged back to 3–2 following goals by Steve Sumner and Steve Woodin, and began to look slightly unsteady as the game wore on. The contest eventually finished 5–2 to Scotland, yet New Zealand had made a real impression in their first-ever game at a World Cup finals. Their last group game in 1982 came against a Brazilian team boasting the talents of Zico and Socrates. It was a sobering end to the All Whites' World Cup debut as they were beaten 4–0.

They return from the international wilderness boasting a more experienced squad, many of whom ply their trade in the European, Asian and Australian leagues. A-League star Shane Smeltz will hope to make a real impression at the finals in 2010; he was New Zealand's top goalscorer during the OFC qualification process, netting eight goals in six games (although he was out-scored by Fiji's prolific Osea Vakatalesau, who scored a staggering 12 goals, albeit in more games), and alongside centre-forward Rory Fallon, is perhaps one of the All Whites' most promising players. The team is captained by Blackburn Rovers' experienced centre-half Ryan Nelsen, who will travel to South Africa with a view to go one better than the team of 1982 and progress through the preliminary group stages.

Below: New Zealand line up for their play-off game against Bahrain in 2009.

Slovakia

World Cup Appearances: *As Czechoslovakia 8 (1934, 38, 54, 58, 62, 70, 82, 90); first appearance as Slovakia*

World Cup Record: *Runners-up (1934, 1962)*

How They Qualified: *Winners UEFA Group 3*

Shirt: *Blue with white trim*

Slovakia booked their first place in a World Cup since gaining independence via a tense victory over Poland in October 2009. Topping their group above neighbours Slovenia, Slovakia progressed out of a very open qualifying group that included eastern European neighbours Poland, Slovenia and the Czech Republic, along with Northern Ireland and San Marino. Despite losing twice and conceding a total of ten goals, Slovakia finished first by just two points and progressed to their first World Cup finals since gaining independence from Czechoslovakia in 1993.

Indeed, Czechoslovakia had a very rich international history which peaked in

Below: Filip Holosko rides the challenge of England defender John Terry.

Above: Marek Sapara begins an attack in the heart of midfield.

1976 when they beat West Germany after extra time in the final of the European Championships in Yugoslavia. Ján Svehlík – a Slovak-born centre-forward who plied his trade at SK Slovan Bratislava – and Karol Dobias put Czechoslovakia in front with two first-half goals, but West Germany pegged the eastern Europeans back with Dieter Müller netting in the first half before Bernd Hölzenbein's 89th-minute strike ensured extra time. The Czechs won on penalties, scoring all five of their spot kicks and lifting the Henri Delaunay Trophy for the first time in their history. It was a culmination of sorts for Czechoslovakia following their World Cup travails in the first 30 years of the competition: they have been runners-up twice, in 1934 when they lost to hosts Italy and again in 1962 when they lost to Brazil in Chile.

Slovakia gained independence in 1993 and played their first game as Slovakia against the United Arab Emirates in 1994. Their first competitive game was a Euro 1996 qualification game against

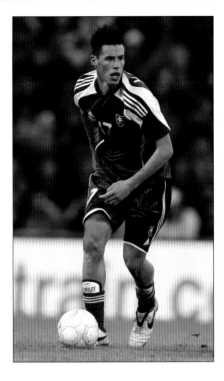

Above: Slovakia captain Marek Hamsik looks for the killer pass.

France which ended 0–0 and was ultimately part of an unsuccessful European Championship qualifying campaign (Slovakia finished third to France and Romania). Despite not qualifying for a European Championship since gaining independence, Slovakia have demonstrated clear potential on the international scene and their determination and organization was rewarded with a coveted place at the finals in South Africa.

Coached by former Czechoslovakia international Vladimir Weiss, the Slovakian team will travel to South Africa expecting to emerge victorious from the group stages. Scoring the most goals in what became a very tight group (with Stanislav Sesták joint top goalscorer with six goals) puts the eastern Europeans in good stead for the finals, and with Robert Vittek spearheading their attack, Slovakia could well be a team to keep an eye on in South Africa. It remains to be seen, however, whether Slovakia can emulate their predecessors and go beyond the preliminary group stages.

Brazil

World Cup Appearances: *18 (1930, 34, 38, 50, 54, 58, 62, 66, 70, 74, 78, 82, 86, 90, 94, 98, 2002, 06)*

World Cup Record: *Winners 5 (1958, 62, 70, 94, 2002); runners-up 2 (1950, 98); third place 2 (1938, 78); fourth place 1 (1974)*

How They Qualified: *Winners CONMEBOL*

Shirt: *Yellow with green trim*

Brazil are quite simply the most successful and entertaining team in the world. The famous yellow jersey of Brazil is a symbol of footballing purity; from a country where football is everything, winning with style whilst playing beautiful football is essential.

Brazil's high reputation was established in the 1950s, when they reached the final in two World Cups. In 1950 the Brazilians crashed 2–1 to Uruguay on home soil. Eight years later Brazil were back in the final with a team boosted by Didi, Garrincha and the 17-year-old Pelé. Brazil's secret weapon was their revolutionary 4–2–4 system. A 5–2 semi-final victory against France, with goals

Below: Brazil dominated international football throughout the 1950s and 1960s. Vava, seen here, was one of the era's greatest players.

from Vava and Didi, and a Pelé hat-trick, ensured passage to the final where hosts Sweden lost to the same score.

In 1962, Brazil successfully defended their world title, with a line-up that included seven members of the team that had beaten France four years earlier. Among the missing was Pelé, whose tournament was curtailed by an injury sustained in the group game against Czechoslovakia. Pelé again found himself on the treatment table after some brutal man-marking against Bulgaria and Portugal in the 1966 World Cup, but this time Brazil struggled to replace their ailing hero and crashed out of the competition at the first hurdle.

The South Americans bounced back and the Brazil line-up of 1970 is widely regarded as the finest attacking team the game has ever seen. From Carlos Alberto in defence to Rivelino and Pelé in attack, the football flowed in breathtaking fashion. After defeating Uruguay in the semi-final, Brazil made light work of overcoming Italy 4–1 in the final. The 1970s and 1980s saw a series of gifted players grace the yellow jersey, but defensive frailties prevented any further addition to their tally of World Cups. The waiting finally came to an end in 1994 when Mario Zagallo's much-maligned team beat Italy on penalties in the final of

Above: The 2007 Ballon D'or winner Kaka is another in a long line of talented Brazilian playmakers.

USA 1994. Four years later, Brazil equalled the West German record by reaching a sixth World Cup final, but despite the presence of star players Rivaldo and Ronaldo, who played after suffering a fit hours before, the reigning South American champions stumbled to a surprise 3–0 defeat.

Five of the players in that match redeemed themselves in 2002, when Brazil won the cup for the fifth time, beating Germany 2–0 in the final. Cafu, the captain, became the first player to appear in the final on three consecutive occasions, and Ronaldo scored both goals to win the Golden Boot with a total of eight. They couldn't defend their title again, however, and in 2006 they lost 1–0 to France in the quarter-finals.

Brazil enter the 2010 finals as favourites after winning both the 2007 Copa America and the 2009 Confederations Cup. With the likes of Dani Alves in defence and Kaka conducting the midfield, they remain the team to avoid in South Africa.

Korea DPR

World Cup Appearances: *1 (1966)*
World Cup Record: *Second round 1 (1966)*
How They Qualified: *Second place AFC Group B*
Shirt: *Red with white trim*

For at least 35 years, Korea DPR's progress to a World Cup quarter-final remained the highest achievement of any Asian team in the competition. In England, in 1966, Korea DPR stunned Italy by beating the Europeans 1–0 to progress to a quarter-final contest against Portugal; it could have become even greater, moreover, as they went on to take a 3-0 lead against Portugal in the next round, only to be beaten 5–3 following a Eusebio-inspired comeback (which included a hat-trick from the Portuguese legend himself).

It was in the same competition in Japan and South Korea some 36 years later that such a massive achievement was bettered, when Korea DPR's neighbours and rivals South Korea progressed to a semi-final showdown with eventual 2002 finalists Germany. Even so, Korea DPR's early achievements shouldn't be overlooked and their progression to the

Below: The competitive Pak Nam-Chol clears the ball out of defence.

quarter-finals in 1966 remains one of the most impressive footballing achievements of the last century.

Today, Korea DPR is made up of players from both the Democratic People's Republic of Korea and players born in Japan. Ranked at number 91 in the world by FIFA, they began their journey to South Africa 2010 with a victory over Mongolia in the first round of Asian qualifying. The long road to qualification concluded with a goalless draw away to Saudi Arabia which secured second place in Group B of Asian qualifying on goal difference and, along with South Korea, a place at the 2010 finals. Significantly, the tournament

Above: Kim Yong-Jun links up play in a friendly away to FC Nantes in 2009.

in South Africa will be the first finals to host both South Korea and Korea DPR.

Coached by Kim Jong-Hun and captained by Nam Song-Chol, DPR Korea are renowned for their organized defence and their flowing, counter-attacking football. Making their first competitive appearance at a World Cup finals since exiting the tournament at Goodison Park in Liverpool, DPR Korea enter the 2010 competition with hopes of reaching the knockout stages, although it is highly unlikely they will better the legendary class of 1966.

Ivory Coast

World Cup Appearances: *1 (2006)*
World Cup Record: *First round (2006)*
How They Qualified: *Winners CAF Group E*
Shirt: *Orange with green trim*

The Côte d'Ivoire are one of the most competitive teams in Africa and are ranked second to Cameroon in CAF's overall ranking system. They finished within the top four in the past two African Nations Cup competitions (runners-up in 2006 and fourth-place finishers in 2008) and are second only to Egypt in the amount of appearances made in the continental competition. With a squad of talented strikers, playmakers and highly experienced defenders, the Ivory Coast will be entering their second World Cup with realistic expectations of bettering their debut appearance in Germany in 2006.

The Ivory Coast's first appearance in the World Cup finals was a rather daunting one. Qualifying for the 2006 World Cup in Germany for the first time in their history, 'Les Éléphants' were drawn in what became known as the 'group of death', which featured

Below: Didier Drogba is one of the best strikers in world football.

Above: The Ivory Coast team line up prior to a World Cup qualifying game against Benin.

seasoned international competitors Argentina and Holland, as well as spirited outsiders Serbia and Montenegro. The Ivory Coast faired well: despite losing to both Argentina and Holland, they recorded a precious win over Serbia and Montenegro, turning a 2–0 deficit into an unlikely 3–2 win following a brace from Aruna Dindane and a winning penalty scored by Bonaventure Kalou.

Since their debut appearance in 2006, Les Éléphants were semi-finalists at the African Nations Cup in 2008 and were represented at the Beijing Olympics, where they lost in the knockout stages to the eventual silver medallists Nigeria. Topping their group without losing a game in the 2010 CAF World Cup qualifying rounds, The Ivory Coast booked their place in the finals after a tense 1–1 draw with Malawi, requiring a goal from substitute Didier Drogba to confirm their place. It was a strong qualifying campaign, with Les Éléphants scoring a cool 19 goals and conceding only 4. They finished above Malawi, Guinea and Burkina Faso, the last of whom scored twice against the Ivory Coast in Ouagadougou, Burkina

Faso, in a fantastic game which Les Éléphants went on finally to win 3–2 in June 2009.

With the highly experienced captain Kolo Toure patrolling the defence alongside the attack-minded Arthur Boka, while seasoned striker Didier Drogba leads the attack, the Ivory Coast will be a force to be reckoned with at the finals in South Africa; with their immense athleticism and spirit, the west Africans are one of the strongest African teams to have ever qualified for a World Cup finals and many will fancy Les Éléphants' chances to progress well beyond the preliminary group stages. As the third African team to qualify for the 2010 finals (following the host's automatic qualification and Ghana's straightforward passage), the Ivory Coast are again looking to demonstrate their full potential and will relish the opportunity to assert their numerous strengths and abilities on the greatest footballing stage in the world.

Portugal

World Cup Appearances: *4 (1966, 86, 2002, 06)*

World Cup Record: *Third place 1 (1966)*

How They Qualified: *UEFA play-off winners*

Shirt: *Red with green trim*

Portugal made their international debut in 1921, but it was not until 1966 that they qualified for their first World Cup finals. The Portugal of 1966 was built around the successful Benfica team of the same era, and had the great Eusebio as its inspiration. Club-mates José Aguas and captain Mario Coluña joined Eusebio, who with nine goals was the tournament's top scorer, in a team that exceeded all expectation by finishing third. They defeated Brazil and Hungary before beating North Korea 5–3 in the quarter-finals. Hosts and eventual winners England beat Portugal in an epic semi-final that ended 2–1.

Below: Eusebio, top scorer at the World Cup finals of 1966.

Above: The sublimely skilful Cristiano Ronaldo will be a key man in Portugal's team at the 2010 World Cup.

After the achievements of 1966, Portugal failed to qualify for the next four World Cup finals, and it was not until the 1980s that they re-emerged as a significant force. At the 1984 European Championships, Portugal fell to hosts France in a memorable semi-final that went to extra time. Two years later the Portuguese were back in the World Cup finals, but despite the addition of the prodigiously talented Paulo Futre, they were eliminated at the group stage.

By the mid-1990s, members of Portugal's all-conquering youth team – 'The Golden Generation' – were beginning to dominate the senior line-up, and at the 1996 European Championships players such as Rui Costa, Luis Figo and Joao Pinto made their mark. Portugal were, according to many pundits, the most entertaining team on show at Euro 1996, although the lack of a convincing centre-forward ultimately proved costly in a run that ended with defeat by the Czech Republic in the semi-finals. Portugal failed to qualify for the 1998 World Cup finals, but lost just one of their games en route to Euro 2000, where they reached the semi-finals.

Portugal were among the favourites at the World Cup in 2002, but in one of the many big upsets of the tournament they lost their opening game, a little unluckily, 3–2 to the USA. Portugal failed to recover their form, and a 1–0 defeat by South Korea meant elimination at the group stage. Hosting Euro 2004, they suffered a bitter disappointment in reaching the final but losing 1–0 to outsiders Greece. A Zinedine Zidane penalty in the semi-final of the 2006 World Cup finals prevented Portugal from reaching their first final, and they were knocked out by Germany in the quarter-final of Euro 2008.

The road to 2010 wasn't as simple as initially expected. Under coach Carlos Queiróz, Portugal struggled to escape their group, which included Sweden and Denmark. They finished second in Group 1 and had to contest a tricky play-off against Bosnia without injured playmaker Cristiano Ronaldo. They won 2–0 on aggregate and progressed to their fifth World Cup appearance since 1966.

Spain

World Cup Appearances: *11 (1938, 50, 66, 78, 82, 86, 90, 94, 98, 2002, 06)*

World Cup Record: *Fourth place 1 (1950)*

How They Qualified: *Winners UEFA Group 5*

Shirt: *Red with yellow trim*

Despite having arguably the world's strongest league and some of its finest players, the Spanish team has nearly always disappointed in the final stages of the leading tournaments. Perhaps this is because Spaniards identify more with the regions in which they were born than with the collection of regions that calls itself Spain.

Spain made its World Cup debut in 1938, beating Brazil before losing to the hosts and eventual winners Italy, in a match that required extra time and a replay. The Spaniards' next World Cup appearance came in 1950, and they again reached the second round. Somewhat surprisingly, given Real Madrid's successes of the 1950s and 1960s, Spain missed the next three tournaments and were eliminated in 1966 at the first

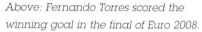

Above: Fernando Torres scored the winning goal in the final of Euro 2008.

hurdle. It is often said that the many foreigners who play in Spain's Primera Liga undermine the progress of the national team, but in the 1960s this argument had little foundation, since a number of the league's imported stars declared for the Spanish red jersey, among them Alfredo Di Stefano, Ferenc Puskas and José Santamaria.

The players that claimed victory at the Bernabeu stadium in the European Championships of 1964, however, were all Spanish-born. The USSR provided the opposition in the final but lost 2–1 to a team managed by José Villalonga, and

inspired by midfielder Luis Suarez. Twenty years later Spain were back in the final of the European Championships, but this time they lost to France 2–0.

At USA 1994 it took a late goal from Italy's Roberto Baggio to end Spanish hopes in the quarter-finals, while at Euro 1996 England required a penalty shoot-out to get past Javier Clemente's team. Four years later, Spain lost to France in the quarter-finals of Euro 2000 in Bruges. Bad luck again caused their exit from the World Cup in 2002, where they were among the favourites. Mistakes in their quarter-final against co-hosts South Korea caused two Spanish goals, including a 'golden goal', to be ruled out, and Spain lost on a penalty shoot-out.

Spain's long wait for a second major trophy came to an end when a first-half goal from Fernando Torres brought them victory over Germany at Euro 2008, and they duly rose to the top of the world rankings. Their quest for a first World Cup success is certainly on course and the team that won Spain's first international trophy for 44 years are determined to cement their reputation as one of the all-time greats during the finals in South Africa in 2010.

Below: Spain celebrate victory at the European Championships in 2008, their second major tournament success.

Switzerland

World Cup Appearances: *8 (1934, 38, 50, 54, 62, 66, 94, 2006)*

World Cup Record: *Quarter-finals 3 (1934, 38, 54)*

How They Qualified: *Winners UEFA Group 2*

Shirt: *Red with white trim*

Switzerland booked their places in the World Cup finals in South Africa after a goalless draw against Israel in October 2009. They finished top of a very tight group which included 2004 European Champions Greece, Israel, Latvia, Luxembourg and Moldova. Their qualification for both the 2006 and 2010 tournaments follows an enduring period of disappointment for the Swiss national team; they qualified only once for the World Cup between 1970 and 2006 – for the finals of USA 1994, where they progressed to the first round of knockout stages – and this is only the third time they've qualified for successive World Cup finals.

Switzerland were a real mainstay of early World Cup finals, however, participating in every tournament between 1934 and 1954. Indeed, this was perhaps their richest era, progressing to three quarter-finals in 1934, '38, and '54 respectively. Despite leaving those finals relatively early, their progression in each tournament is quite remarkable given they were knocked out twice by beaten finalists – Czechoslovakia in 1934 and Hungary in 1938 – and were beaten 7–5 on home turf against neighbours Austria in 1954.

Switzerland failed to reappear in a World Cup since losing to Austria in 1954 until they gained a qualification berth for the 1994 tournament held in the USA. They reached the first round of the knockout stages, losing to Spain 3–0 in Washington. Qualification for the finals in 1998 and 2002 was unsuccessful, but they managed to qualify for the tournament in Germany four years later. Drawing France, Togo

Above: Valon Behrami is a creative force in central midfield.

and South Korea in their group, Switzerland secured a place in the second round by beating both Togo and South Korea 2–0. They met Ukraine in the second round, losing on penalties after a goalless draw.

Nevertheless, there is real belief in the current generation of Swiss internationals: Alexander Frei – the country's captain and Switzerland's top scorer at the 2006 World Cup – remains the focal point for the Swiss attack alongside Hakan Yakin, and there is a decent amount of talent in both midfield and defence. The team is currently coached by Ottmar Hitzfeld, the former German international striker, and proven winner of silverware at club level. Whether the veteran manager can also find success at international level remains to be seen, and many expect Switzerland to struggle to emerge from their group.

Left: Hakan Yakin celebrates a decisive goal against Turkey in 2006.

Chile

World Cup Appearances: *7 (1930, 50, 62, 66, 74, 82, 98)*

World Cup Record: *Third place 1 (1962); second round 1 (1998)*

How They Qualified: *Second place CONMEBOL*

Shirt: *Red with white trim*

Chile's status within world football enjoyed something of a renaissance during the late 1990s, and they entered the 21st century as South America's fourth team. Chile, whose population of 14 million seems insignificant alongside rivals Brazil (154 million), Mexico (93 million) and Argentina (35 million), progressed to the semi-finals of the 1999 Copa America, and they were regarded as a significant threat to the dominance of Argentina and Brazil.

Below: Marcelo Salas scores Chile's equalizer against Italy at the 1998 World Cup finals in France.

Chile's progress at the end of the 20th century was in stark contrast to their early days in international football. The national team made its debut against Argentina in 1910, losing 3–1, to begin a run of defeats that extended for 13 games and nine years. Chile had to wait even longer for a first victory, success arriving in fine style with the 7–1 trouncing of Bolivia in 1926.

After their slow start, a slight upturn in fortune saw Chile become a regular feature of the World Cup after World War II. However, it was not until 1962 that they progressed beyond the first round. Chile, then hosts, finished the tournament in third place after losing to eventual champions Brazil in the semi-finals. The shameful scenes during their violent group match with Italy, however, overshadowed the achievement. The so-called 'Battle of Santiago' ended with two Italians being sent off, and although Chile won the game 2–0, they emerged with little credit

Above: Striker Ivan Zamorano, a key member of Nelson Acosta's Chilean line-up of the 1990s.

from the most brutal match in the history of the World Cup finals.

During the 1970s and 1980s, Chile progressed to two Copa America finals, but were defeated both times, and it was not until the late 1990s that they regained their status as serious contenders. The team of the 1990s, managed by Nelson Acosta, was built around the strike partnership of Ivan Zamorano and Marcelo Salas and, after a series of impressive results, rose to ninth place in FIFA's rankings prior to the 1998 World Cup finals in France. For the second time in their history, Chile progressed to the second round of the competition but, as in 1962, were defeated 4–1 by Brazil.

A dip in form saw the team miss the 2002 and 2006 finals, but a stronger Chile finished second in the qualifying group for the 2010 tournament and will travel to South Africa hoping to emulate the achievements of 1962.

Honduras

World Cup Appearances: *1 (1982)*
World Cup Record: *First round 1 (1982)*
How They Qualified: *Third place CONCACAF*
Shirt: *White*

'Los Catrachos' confirmed their place at their second World Cup in October 2009, following a 1–0 win against El Salvador which guaranteed a top three finish in the final CONCACAF qualification table. Their only previous World Cup appearance was in 1982 when they finished bottom of a group featuring Northern Ireland, Yugoslavia and tournament hosts Spain. Los Catrachos registered two draws and one defeat during their World Cup debut and would have to wait nearly three decades before they could prove themselves again on the world's foremost international stage.

Below: Carlos Palacios shrugs off the challenge of Haiti's Brunel Eucien.

The 2001 Copa America tournament proved to be the springboard for the current renaissance in Honduran international football. After replacing Argentina at the continental tournament due to a last-minute change of heart by the Argentine FA, Honduras progressed to the semi-finals after knocking out South American giants Brazil in an amazing 2–0 win. Despite failing to qualify for the 2002 and 2006 World Cup finals (by only three points in 2002), Honduras consolidated their position as one of the best teams in the CONCACAF zone after qualifying in third place for the 2010 World Cup finals in South Africa.

Captained by the veteran attacking midfielder Amado Guevara – who is the most capped player in the country's

Above: The attacking midfielder Walter Martinez attempts to bring the ball under control.

history – and spearheaded by the prolific Carlos Pavon, Honduras will be seen as real underdogs in South Africa 2010. Despite boasting numerous experienced players from most top European and South American leagues, including midfield anchor Wilson Palacios who currently plies his trade at Tottenham Hotspur in the English Premier League, Honduras will be an unknown quantity for many international teams, and it remains to be seen whether they have enough not only to register their first-ever World Cup victory but also to progress beyond the group stages in South Africa in 2010.

World Cup 2010: Results

GROUP A

J'BURG ▪ FRI 11 JUNE ▪ 16:00 (LOCAL TIME, 2 HOURS AHEAD OF BST)

☐ **S. AFRICA**   SCORERS: _____
☐ **MEXICO**   SCORERS: _____

CAPE TOWN ▪ FRI 11 JUNE ▪ 20:30

☐ **URUGUAY**   SCORERS: _____
☐ **FRANCE**   SCORERS: _____

TSHWANE/PRETORIA ▪ WED 16 JUNE ▪ 20:30

☐ **S. AFRICA**   SCORERS: _____
☐ **URUGUAY**   SCORERS: _____

POLOKWANE ▪ THURS 17 JUNE ▪ 20:30

☐ **FRANCE**   SCORERS: _____
☐ **MEXICO**   SCORERS: _____

RUSTENBURG ▪ TUES 22 JUNE ▪ 16:00

☐ **MEXICO**   SCORERS: _____
☐ **URUGUAY**   SCORERS: _____

MANGAUNG/BLOEMFONTEIN ▪ TUES 22 JUNE ▪ 16:00

☐ **FRANCE**   SCORERS: _____
☐ **S. AFRICA**   SCORERS: _____

Group A Final Table	W	D	L	F	A	Pts

GROUP C

RUSTENBURG ▪ SAT 12 JUNE ▪ 20:30

☐ **ENGLAND**   SCORERS: _____
☐ **USA**   SCORERS: _____

POLOKWANE ▪ SUN 13 JUNE ▪ 13:30

☐ **ALGERIA**   SCORERS: _____
☐ **SLOVENIA**   SCORERS: _____

JOHANNESBURG ▪ FRI 18 JUNE ▪ 16:00

☐ **SLOVENIA**   SCORERS: _____
☐ **USA**   SCORERS: _____

CAPE TOWN ▪ FRI 18 JUNE ▪ 16:00

☐ **ENGLAND**   SCORERS: _____
☐ **ALGERIA**   SCORERS: _____

NELSON MANDELA BAY/PORT ELIZABETH ▪ WED 23 JUNE ▪ 16:00

☐ **SLOVENIA**   SCORERS: _____
☐ **ENGLAND**   SCORERS: _____

TSHWANE/PRETORIA ▪ WED 23 JUNE ▪ 16:00

☐ **USA**   SCORERS: _____
☐ **ALGERIA**   SCORERS: _____

Group C Final Table	W	D	L	F	A	Pts

GROUP B

JOHANNESBURG ▪ SAT 12 JUNE ▪ 16:00

☐ **ARGENTINA**   SCORERS: _____
☐ **NIGERIA**   SCORERS: _____

NELSON MANDELA BAY/PORT ELIZABETH ▪ SAT 12 JUNE ▪ 13:30

☐ **S. KOREA**   SCORERS: _____
☐ **GREECE**   SCORERS: _____

MANGAUNG/BLOEMFONTEIN ▪ THU 17 JUNE ▪ 16:00

☐ **GREECE**   SCORERS: _____
☐ **NIGERIA**   SCORERS: _____

JOHANNESBURG ▪ THU 17 JUNE ▪ 13:30

☐ **ARGENTINA**   SCORERS: _____
☐ **S. KOREA**   SCORERS: _____

DURBAN ▪ TUE 22 JUNE ▪ 20:30

☐ **NIGERIA**   SCORERS: _____
☐ **S. KOREA**   SCORERS: _____

POLOKWANE ▪ TUE 22 JUNE ▪ 20:30

☐ **GREECE**   SCORERS: _____
☐ **ARGENTINA**   SCORERS: _____

Group B Final Table	W	D	L	F	A	Pts

GROUP D

DURBAN ▪ SUN 13 JUNE ▪ 20:30

☐ **GERMANY**   SCORERS: _____
☐ **AUSTRALIA**   SCORERS: _____

TSHWANE/PRETORIA ▪ SUN 13 JUNE ▪ 16:00

☐ **SERBIA**   SCORERS: _____
☐ **GHANA**   SCORERS: _____

NELSON MANDELA BAY/PORT ELIZABETH ▪ FRI 18 JUNE ▪ 13:30

☐ **GERMANY**   SCORERS: _____
☐ **SERBIA**   SCORERS: _____

RUSTENBURG ▪ SAT 19 JUNE ▪ 16:00

☐ **GHANA**   SCORERS: _____
☐ **AUSTRALIA**   SCORERS: _____

JOHANNESBURG ▪ WED 23 JUNE ▪ 20:30

☐ **GHANA**   SCORERS: _____
☐ **GERMANY**   SCORERS: _____

NELSPRUIT ▪ WED 23 JUNE ▪ 20:30

☐ **AUSTRALIA**   SCORERS: _____
☐ **SERBIA**   SCORERS: _____

Group D Final Table	W	D	L	F	A	Pts

GROUP E

JOHANNESBURG ▪ MON 14 JUNE ▪ 13:30
☐ HOLLAND   SCORERS: _____
☐ DENMARK   SCORERS: _____

MANGAUNG/BLOEMFONTEIN ▪ MON 14 JUNE ▪ 16:00
☐ JAPAN   SCORERS: _____
☐ CAMEROON   SCORERS: _____

DURBAN ▪ SAT 19 JUNE ▪ 13:30
☐ HOLLAND   SCORERS: _____
☐ JAPAN   SCORERS: _____

TSHWANE/PRETORIA ▪ SAT 19 JUNE ▪ 20:30
☐ CAMEROON   SCORERS: _____
☐ DENMARK   SCORERS: _____

RUSTENBURG ▪ THURS 24 JUNE ▪ 20:30
☐ DENMARK   SCORERS: _____
☐ JAPAN   SCORERS: _____

CAPE TOWN ▪ THURS 24 JUNE ▪ 20:30
☐ CAMEROON   SCORERS: _____
☐ HOLLAND   SCORERS: _____

Group E Final Table	W	D	L	F	A	Pts

GROUP G

NELSON MANDELA BAY/PORT ELIZABETH ▪ TUE 15 JUNE ▪ 16:00
☐ I. COAST   SCORERS: _____
☐ PORTUGAL   SCORERS: _____

JOHANNESBURG ▪ TUE 15 JUNE ▪ 20:30
☐ BRAZIL   SCORERS: _____
☐ KOREA DPR   SCORERS: _____

JOHANNESBURG ▪ SUN 20 JUNE ▪ 20:30
☐ BRAZIL   SCORERS: _____
☐ I. COAST   SCORERS: _____

CAPE TOWN ▪ MON 21 JUNE ▪ 13:30
☐ KOREA DPR   SCORERS: _____
☐ PORTUGAL   SCORERS: _____

DURBAN ▪ FRI 25 JUNE ▪ 16:00
☐ PORTUGAL   SCORERS: _____
☐ BRAZIL   SCORERS: _____

NELSPRUIT ▪ FRI 25 JUNE ▪ 16:00
☐ KOREA DPR   SCORERS: _____
☐ I. COAST   SCORERS: _____

Group G Final Table	W	D	L	F	A	Pts

GROUP F

CAPE TOWN ▪ MON 14 JUNE ▪ 20:30
☐ ITALY   SCORERS: _____
☐ PARAGUAY   SCORERS: _____

RUSTENBURG ▪ TUE 15 JUNE ▪ 13:30
☐ N. ZEALAND   SCORERS: _____
☐ SLOVAKIA   SCORERS: _____

MANGAUNG/BLOEMFONTEIN ▪ SUN 20 JUNE ▪ 13:30
☐ SLOVAKIA   SCORERS: _____
☐ PARAGUAY   SCORERS: _____

NELSPRUIT ▪ SUN 20 JUNE ▪ 16:00
☐ ITALY   SCORERS: _____
☐ N. ZEALAND   SCORERS: _____

JOHANNESBURG ▪ THURS 24 JUNE ▪ 16:00
☐ SLOVAKIA   SCORERS: _____
☐ ITALY   SCORERS: _____

POLOKWANE ▪ THURS 24 JUNE ▪ 16:00
☐ PARAGUAY   SCORERS: _____
☐ N. ZEALAND   SCORERS: _____

Group F Final Table	W	D	L	F	A	Pts

GROUP H

NELSPRUIT ▪ WED 16 JUNE ▪ 13:30
☐ HONDURAS   SCORERS: _____
☐ CHILE   SCORERS: _____

DURBAN ▪ WED 16 JUNE ▪ 16:00
☐ SPAIN   SCORERS: _____
☐ SWITZERLAND   SCORERS: _____

NELSON MANDELA BAY/PORT ELIZABETH ▪ MON 21 JUNE ▪ 16:00
☐ CHILE   SCORERS: _____
☐ SWITZERLAND   SCORERS: _____

JOHANNESBURG ▪ MON 21 JUNE ▪ 20:30
☐ SPAIN   SCORERS: _____
☐ HONDURAS   SCORERS: _____

TSHWANE/PRETORIA ▪ FRI 25 JUNE ▪ 20:30
☐ CHILE   SCORERS: _____
☐ SPAIN   SCORERS: _____

MANGAUNG/BLOEMFONTEIN ▪ FRI 25 JUNE ▪ 20:30
☐ SWITZERLAND   SCORERS: _____
☐ HONDURAS   SCORERS: _____

Group H Final Table	W	D	L	F	A	Pts

SECOND ROUND

GAME 1 ▪ N. MANDELA BAY/PORT ELIZABETH ▪ 26 JUNE ▪ 16:00

☐ .... SCORERS: _____

☐ .... SCORERS: _____

GAME 2 ▪ RUSTENBURG ▪ 26 JUNE ▪ 20:30

☐ .... SCORERS: _____

☐ .... SCORERS: _____

GAME 3 ▪ MANGAUNG/BLOEMFONTEIN ▪ 27 JUNE ▪ 16:00

☐ .... SCORERS: _____

☐ .... SCORERS: _____

GAME 4 ▪ JOHANNESBURG ▪ 27 JUNE ▪ 20:30

☐ .... SCORERS: _____

☐ .... SCORERS: _____

GAME 5 ▪ DURBAN ▪ 28 JUNE ▪ 16:00

☐ .... SCORERS: _____

☐ .... SCORERS: _____

GAME 6 ▪ JOHANNESBURG ▪ 28 JUNE ▪ 20:30

☐ .... SCORERS: _____

☐ .... SCORERS: _____

GAME 7 ▪ TSHWANE/PRETORIA ▪ 29 JUNE ▪ 16:00

☐ .... SCORERS: _____

☐ .... SCORERS: _____

GAME 8 ▪ CAPE TOWN ▪ 29 JUNE ▪ 20:30

☐ .... SCORERS: _____

☐ .... SCORERS: _____

QUARTER-FINALS

GAME A ▪ N. MANDELA BAY/PORT ELIZABETH ▪ 02 JULY ▪ 16:00

☐ .... SCORERS: _____

☐ .... SCORERS: _____

GAME C ▪ JOHANNESBURG ▪ 02 JULY ▪ 20:30

☐ .... SCORERS: _____

☐ .... SCORERS: _____

GAME B ▪ CAPE TOWN ▪ 03 JULY ▪ 16:00

☐ .... SCORERS: _____

☐ .... SCORERS: _____

GAME D ▪ JOHANNESBURG ▪ 03 JULY ▪ 20:30

☐ .... SCORERS: _____

☐ .... SCORERS: _____

SEMI-FINALS

GAME 1 ▪ CAPE TOWN ▪ 06 JULY ▪ 20:30

☐ .... SCORERS: _____

☐ .... SCORERS: _____

GAME 2 ▪ DURBAN ▪ 07 JULY ▪ 20:30

☐ .... SCORERS: _____

☐ .... SCORERS: _____

Subs

Subs

Subs

Subs

THIRD PLACE PLAY-OFF

NELSON MANDELA BAY/PORT ELIZABETH ▪ 10 JULY ▪ 20:30

☐ .... SCORERS: _____   ☐ .... SCORERS: _____

THE FINAL

JOHANNESBURG ▪ 11 JULY ▪ 20:30

☐ .... SCORERS: _____   ☐ .... SCORERS: _____

Subs

Subs

PENALTY TAKERS

☐ _____
☐ _____
☐ _____
☐ _____
☐ _____
☐ _____
☐ _____
☐ _____
☐ _____
☐ _____

PENALTY TAKERS

☐ _____
☐ _____
☐ _____
☐ _____
☐ _____
☐ _____
☐ _____
☐ _____
☐ _____
☐ _____

REFEREE

_____

ASSISTANT REFEREES

_____

_____

Index

Africa (CAF) 22, 27
Algeria 16, 22, 23
    World Cup 2010 38
America, Central and North
    (CONCACAF) 22, 27
America, South
    (CONMEBOL) 22–3, 27
Argentina 8, 9, 10, 13, 15, 17,
    18, 19, 21, 23
    World Cup 2010 32
Asia (AFC) 22, 27
Australia 22, 27
    World Cup 2010 41

Bahrain 22, 23
Ballack, Michael 40
Belgium 8, 17, 19
Brazil 8, 9, 10, 11, 12–13, 14,
    15, 16, 17, 18–19, 20, 21,
    22, 23, 27
    World Cup 2010 52

Cahill, Tim 41
Cannavaro, Fabio 48
Cameroon 16, 18, 21, 22
    World Cup 2010 47
Chile 10, 12, 22, 23, 27
    World Cup 2010 58
Colombia 17, 19, 23
Costa Rica 18, 21, 22, 23
Croatia 19
Czechoslovakia 8, 9, 10, 12

Denmark
    World Cup 2010 45
Donovan, Landon 37

DPR Korea 13, 20, 22
    World Cup 2010 53
Drogba, Didier 54
Dutch East Indies 9

Ecuador 21, 23
Egypt 4, 22, 23
El Salvador 16
England 10, 12–13, 14, 17, 18,
    19, 20, 21, 22, 27
    World Cup 2010 36
Essien, Michael, 43
Eto'o, Samuel 47
Europe (UEFA) 22, 27 19

FIFA 4, 8, 16, 17, 20
Forlan, Diego 30
France 8, 9, 10, 11, 16–17, 18,
    19, 20, 21, 22, 23
    World Cup 2010 31

Germany 4, 5, 8, 18, 19, 20–1,
    27
    West Germany 10, 11, 12, 13,
        14, 15, 16–17
    World Cup 2010 40
Ghana 21, 22, 27
    World Cup 2010 43
Greece 23
    World Cup 2010 35

Henry, Thierry 31
Holland 8, 14–15, 18, 19, 21, 22
    World Cup 2010 44
Honduras 16, 22
    World Cup 2010 59
Hungary 9, 10, 13

Hurst, Geoff 7, 13
Italy 4, 5, 8, 9, 12, 13, 14, 15,
    16, 17, 18, 19, 21, 27
    World Cup 2010 48
Ivory Coast 22
    World Cup 2010 54

Japan 20
    World Cup 2010 46

Kaka 52

Lampard, Frank 36

Maradona, Diego 7, 17, 19, 23,
    32
Messi, Lionel 32
Mexico 8, 12, 14, 17, 22
    World Cup 2010 29
Morocco 4

New Caledonia 22
New Zealand 16, 22, 23
    World Cup 2010 50
Nigeria 22
    World Cup 2010 33
Northern Ireland 16

Oceania (OFC) 22, 27

Paraguay 8, 22, 23
    World Cup 2010 49
Park, Ji-Sung 34
Pelé, Edison Arantes do
    Nascimento 7, 11, 12, 13,
    14, 15
Poland 15, 16
Portugal 10, 13, 20, 21, 22, 23
    World Cup 2010 55

Republic of Ireland 23
Rimet, Jules 9
Robben, Arjen 44
Romania 8, 19
Ronaldo, Cristiano 55
Rooney, Wayne 36
Russia 19, 23

Sanchez, Hugo 29
Saudi Arabia 19, 22
Scotland 10, 18

Senegal 20, 21
Serbia 22
    World Cup 2010 42
Slovakia 27
    World Cup 2010 51
Slovenia 23
    World Cup 2010 39
South Africa 4–5, 7, 22
    World Cup 2010 28
South Korea 20, 22
    World Cup 2010 34
Spain 8, 10, 15, 20, 22, 27
    World Cup 2010 56
Sweden 8, 10, 11, 18
Switzerland 8, 10, 21, 22
    World Cup 2010 57

Torres, Fernando 56

Ukraine 21
Uruguay 4, 8, 9, 10, 14, 22, 23
    World Cup 2010 30
USA 8, 10, 19, 20, 21, 22, 27
    World Cup 2010 37
USSR (Soviet Union) 12, 13

Vanuatu 22

World Cup 2010
    The Qualifiers 20–1
    Qualifying Results 22–3
    Results 62–3

Yakubu, 33
Yugoslavia 8, 10, 12

Zidane, Zinedine 21, 31